THE ACT OF CHANGE

*9 Acts of Change helping you to
Co-create the
Person you were destined to be!*

Dr. Angelo Reynolds, Sr.

The Act of Change

Acts of Change helping you create the person you were destined to be!

By Dr. A.D. Reynolds

P.O. Box 1672
White Plains, Maryland 20695

All RIGHTS RESERVED

No part of this book may be reproduced or transmitted in any form or by any means-electronic or mechanical, including photocopying, recording or any information storage and retrieved system without written permission from the author, except for the inclusion of brief quotations in a review.

The publication is designed to provide accurate and authoritative information, in regard to the subject matter covered. It is sold with the understanding that the Publisher is not engaged in rendering legal, accounting or other professional services. If legal advice or other expert assistance is required, the services of a competent professional person should be sought.

Dr. A.D. Reynolds books are available at special discounts for bulk purchases, sales, promotions, fund raising or educational purposes.

© Copyright 2009 by Dr. A.D. Reynolds

Dedication

To Grandma Taylor who truly showed me how change starts within. Thank you for all you did for us all. I now understand what it meant to develop that covenant with the creator. We will miss you but we know that God had the final resting place for you.

With most gracious Love
Angelo

Kevin Adair, thank-you for your gracious and sincere financial contributions. I'm not sure how long it would have taken for me to finally go to print without your help. Its brothers like you who we need more of in the world to help those in need.

Contents

Dedication		3
Preface		7
Chapter 1	Act 1:	
	Develop a personal covenant with God	11
	Choosing to obey God in faith	13
	Increase Faith by trusting and relying on God	17
	Begin with the end in mind	23
	Attitude is everything	27
	Spirituality Plays a Major Part, Too	30
	Prayer or Meditation	31
	Bible study	32
	Worship and Fellowship	33
	Plant an Abundant Spiritual Harvest	37
Chapter 2	Act 2:	
	Create Personal Picture	38
	Adolescent Identity vs. Role Confusion	38
	The Best is yet to come	44
	It's not where you start, but where you finish	48
	The Past should not dictate your future	49
	The Vitality of Your Personal Picture	51
Chapter 3 Act 3:		
	Identify Your Challenges Barriers Change	55
	The Challenge is yours	65
	Get out of the Comfort zone	68
	Put on Your Armored Gear	69
	Limited Pitfalls	71

Chapter 4	Act 4:	
	Finding Your Life with Purpose	73
	Discovering Your Purpose can define you	81
Chapter 5	Act 5:	
	Program Your Mind for Success	84
	Failure is not an option, it's a choice!	92
	Creating the mindset of self-motivation	96
	Creating the self-talk motivation	100
Chapter 6	Act 6:	
	Use the setbacks as a setup to Comeback	108
Chapter 7	Act 7:	
	Each One Reach One	129
	The act of collectivism	132
	Start thinking about ways to give back	134
	Why not volunteer at our detention centers?	137
Chapter 8	Act 8:	
	Use the past as a catalyst for your future	139
Chapter 9	Act 9:	
	Do You!	146
	Mental vs. emotional thoughts	150
	Spiritual Problems have spiritual solution	152
	Spiritual	153
	Conclusion	156

"Change the way you look at things and the things you look at will change...."

-Dr. Wayne Dyer

"There is nothing like returning to a place that remains unchanged to find the ways in which you yourself have altered...."

-Nelson Mandela

Preface

Some people go through an entire life without change. They come up with every excuse in the world about why they have failed and never achieved their full potential and success in life. These are the same individuals that shouda, coulda, woulda, and never did anything. These are the same cynical people who find fault in everybody, including themselves and someone else, and their alibi is always the blaming game. These are truly the people that can find fault in Jesus Christ! Now we know that Jesus was the only person that was perfect, but somehow these people will find something wrong with Christ.

If you are reading this book, of course, you may not be one of those individuals that I am discussing. You may not be that person because you have made the changes in your life and have no need for any further change. You know that change is needed, but your comfort zone has prohibited you from living that dream, pursuing that passion, or getting the maximum potential that life has to offer you.

However, I am writing today about change because it is vital for almost every part of our lives. It is a universal concept that is inevitable. Although most of us are aware that there is something in our lives that we need to change, most of us don't do it. And here are a few reasons why: fear of being different, getting out of our comfort zone, getting out of our complacency, and not letting go of the past. You know the saying, "If it ain't broken, then don't fix it." The problem with that statement is it does not allow room for change – period! That means that you are going to live your life the same way forever! Not only is that crazy and insane, but disastrous, too!

Because life is full of obstacles and challenges that we cannot solely escape, change should serve as a prerequisite to growth. Unfortunately, many people are stuck at certain places in life because they have no desire to change. One thing is certain about life; it is truly a transformation period. That is, we go through various changes whether we want to or not. Some of the changes that will occur throughout our lives are relationships, health, financial, career, and spiritual changes. Some of those changes can be more difficult to adjust to while others may seem more trivial as we transform through that change. Certainly, these are transformation periods that are going to come.

What I want you to get out of this book is how imperative change is and the impact it can have on your life forever. If you choose to reject change, you are choosing to limit yourself and others around you – especially those people that are important to you, such as family, friends, and coworkers.

As you continue to read this book, I ask you to walk with me as we change the way you think, act, and feel about life. You have the power and ability to take on any challenge, defeat any obstacle, and reach any goal that you set; however, you have to be open to change. God gave each and every one of us the power to make rational decisions, to make sound judgment, and to possess a brain that will be open to change.

As you read this book, I want you to try and bring yourself out of your comfort zone. I know it is difficult, but remember, change is difficult. And if you don't voluntarily come out of that comfort zone, change will ultimately force you out. Begin to think, feel, and act differently about taking on the challenges, obstacles, and setbacks that come your way. And remember, they are never as bad as they seem; they are just life's changes and everyone goes through them.

There are 9 acts that I have created to help you transition with your change. These are acts that I have personally used to make the necessary changes both in my personal and professional life. More importantly, God also gave you the ability to apply these acts; however, many of us refuse to use them. I would like to caution you that these acts are not cardinal rules, just good principles that can be used universally. But I promise you that if you use them and use them wisely, they can be the most powerful principles ever.

And if you are a person who is already utilizing these principles, I suggest you pass them to someone else who you feel could benefit. As we will discuss later, the best gift we can give is that of personal service. And remember that regardless of what you have gone through or are currently going through, the best is still yet to come. Nothing and no one can stop you from making the necessary changes to reach your full, God-given potential!

—Dr. A.D. Reynolds

Act 1
Develop a Personal Covenant with God

"Whoever sheds the blood of man,
By man shall his blood be shed;
For in the image of God has God made man"

Genesis 7:9

The word *covenant* is defined as an agreement between two parties; a solemn promise or vow, especially between God and people. It is the most important personal relationship that you can ever have. There is nothing more important than developing a personal relationship with God. That relationship is infinite. Ask yourself, have you been missing out on the most important things in life? If so, you can do something about it. It's your choice and you are as close to God as you choose to be, just as Abraham's covenant was with God, as He appeared to Abraham in a vision.

God told Abraham, "Do not be afraid, Abram. I am your shield, your very great reward." God accepted Abraham not because he led a perfect life, but because of his responsiveness to God's promises. God looked for faith in Abraham, not moral perfection. No one on this God-given earth is morally righteous; therefore, you will sin, make mistakes, and do things that are against the will of God. The right thing to try and do is walk with faith and the spirit will allow you to overcome life challenges, setbacks, and obstacles…guaranteed!

Think back for a moment when you did something that you knew was against the word of God. You tried, but you sinned anyway. And He knew that you would sin even before you actually did it. Of course you repented, but God forgave you and in most instances blesses you abundantly even though you did not deserve it. That's because He wants you to establish a covenant with Him. You may know Him, but He blesses you enough to show you that if you include Him in all your life's decisions, life will be much easier to handle. You won't lose your sanity because you know God has your back; even when life seems endless and there is no way out of your situation, He will get you through it. Not convinced yet? Just try it. I guarantee that it is one relationship that you will never be sorry that you developed.

Getting closer to God is not as difficult as it may seem. Just as you have formed relationships in the past with friends, you, too, can develop a personal relationship with God. Like any relationship, you must work at it. Think for a moment of those relationships that you have formed in the past that ended up as a waste of time and were not useful to you or anything that you tried to do in life – those persons who deceived you, killed your dreams, and ridiculed you in every way possible to bring your self-esteem or image down. You put your all in them, but they still failed you. Guess what? God never fails at anything, nor does he put people in your life to harm you. The problem is, many times we overlook people, situations, and more importantly, don't pray and ask God before we develop relationships with people, go into business, or make life decisions.

Somehow man thinks that he can outsmart God. It will not happen. He is the ultimate decision maker in your life, but you have to develop that personal relationship with Him. It will not happen by coincidence or luck, but through your personal commitment, dedication, desire, energy, and honesty, you can develop that closeness with God. Honesty is the key. Your choice to be honest with yourself and God is the first step toward that closer relationship with Him. No one will ever be perfect. Jesus' disciples in the Bible were not perfect. In fact, God does not expect us to even try to become perfect, just do the best that we can.

Personally, it took years for me to realize what God was trying to tell me. But like many of us, I was too stubborn, unreceptive to change, and thought that I could do things alone. Let me remind you, *"Through Christ, all things are possible!"* Don't ever lose sight of that. Once I realized that I could not do it alone, I then began to develop that covenant with Him. And just think many of us have the audacity to make God wait. God does not have to wait for anyone. He is a jealous but patient God. And He does everything on His time, not yours. It wasn't until I fully surrendered to Him and developed that covenant that things really began to turn around for me (later I will discuss this).

Choosing to obey God in faith
Deuteronomy 28

Have you ever paid attention to the fact that some points in your life appear to be going smoother than other times have? Or some struggles are less severe and never as bad as they seem? As you know, life can be an emotional roller coaster. These emotional ups and downs clearly can create a level of stress that can be overwhelming for the average person. Nevertheless, choosing to obey God and believe that He has a better way is the solution to all your problems. Some people go through their lives and never realize the power of obeying God's word. They are the same people that believe that things happen by chance or luck. I am here to tell you that there is no such thing as luck, coincidence, or chance. It's all up to your obedience to God and your willingness to follow His words.

Likewise, if you fail to obey His commands, you will be cursed when you go out into the world. You will be defeated by your enemies and no good will come upon you because you did not obey the Lord. Think back for a moment to times when everything appeared to be going wrong. If it wasn't one thing, it was another – a series of trials and tribulations. And each time, they appeared to get worse. It was really like your life was a living hell. And I have heard people say just that. In fact, I have experienced the same thing. On many occasions, I have done the total opposite of what God intended me to do and failed every time. It was not until I made a conscious effort and decision to do exactly what He intended for me did I realize what was truly happening. That is not to say that life will not be a challenge and you won't have any setbacks or obstacles, but when you have a covenant with God, you will be able to deal with them.

If you fully obey the Lord, your God, and carefully follow all his commands I give you today, the Lord God will set you high above all the nations on earth. All blessings will come upon you and accompany you if you obey the Lord, your God. Simply put, do good get good. It's called being obedient to the word of God. It is something so fundamental yet daunting for many people to obey. We tend to do the total opposite. In fact, it's almost like we become rebellious to the mere commands that God has for us. Even when we are disobedient, He still blesses us, knowing that we truly are not deserving of it.

Every time you trust God's wisdom and guidance and do whatever he says, you strengthen your relationship with Him. If God sends you a message, you must respond and act on it. All too many times, we ignore the messages and blessings from God. He answers our prayers and warns us of dangers that are forthcoming. And in many instances, we overlook or shadow the mere facts and miss out on the great blessings that He gives us. If you love God, then you should obey Him. He knows what's best for us, so why not trust in Him with all your heart? If we have been forgiven for our sins by God, why do we have such a difficult time obeying Him? Is it that we think we can do things in life without Him? Or have we become so egotistical that we are now non-believers that God really does what He says He can do?

In the past, some of you have questioned your faith and relationship with God. You say that you believe that all things are possible through Him, but your actions respond differently. You go to church, pay your tithes and offerings, and call yourself a Christian, but the honesty lies in your personal relationship with God. Not to undermine your dedication as a Christian, but anyone can go to church, pay tithes and offerings, and call themselves a Christian. The real test is between you and God. Are you receiving His guidance, His messages, obeying his requests, and doing what He has called you to do?

I can speak personally and answer those questions for you. For a long time, I was resistant to changing and developing a personal relationship with God. I thought that I had it all figured out. Yeah, I always believed in Him, but I never really had a personal relationship with Him until recently. It was almost scary for me because the messages from God had been coming to me for years. Through people, situations, and the angels sent from God, messages about what God wanted me to do for Him were ignored. I am not sure why I ignored those messages, but I finally realized over the years that if I didn't obey God's messages, then He would use someone else to do His work. Can you believe that I had the audacity to have God wait on me to accept the responsibility of doing His work? I truly believe that God chooses some of us to do His work.

On several different occasions, God used people and situations to send messages to me. He first sent a message to me by my oldest child through a dream. One morning, my son was eating breakfast and said, "Dad, Jesus told me to tell you to stay focused and keep doing what you are doing." So I asked him, "Son, what did Jesus look like in your dream?" I thought maybe he had heard this in school or saw it on TV. Then I realized that public schools no longer discuss religion and that he actually talked to Jesus in his dream. He described Jesus as a man with long hair wearing a long robe and without shoes on.

As he described him, I thought, this must be true. Every time I asked my son on several occasions, he would describe Jesus the same and would translate the message to me verbatim. I thought to myself, wow! This is powerful, but I still did not actually follow that message. I allowed social forces (drinking and smoking) to take over as a way to combat my problems. The enemy (Satan) was clearly winning the battle between me and what God wanted me to do. And that is what many people have done. They allow the enemy to destroy them and keep them from developing that relationship with God. And I now totally take accountability for that. The devil will only win if you stop fighting.

On a different occasion, God sent an unknown man to me in a dream. He told the man to tell me that He took me away from the car business because he wanted me to focus on writing and selling my books to help those in need of life changes. I had a car business that went under due to lack of residual cash flow. God took the business away from me because He had another plan for me and I still was not receptive to the message. Can you believe that? I was not doing what God wanted me to do. Like many people who refuse to obey God, there is an ultimate price for not being obedient

Finally, when I was going through one of the toughest periods in my life (that I will discuss in another chapter), my grandmother came to me in another dream with another message. Grandma said to me, "Son, God has sent me to you with a message. He said that he wants you to work for Him." I was again stunned! I marveled to myself that all these times I had not been receptive to God and He was still trying to use me to do his work. I could not figure this one out. And that is the power of what God can and will do for you. Many times, we don't understand things that happen to us in life; however, God has a reason for everything that happens to us and for us in life.

Now this time, I decided to do exactly what He wanted me to do. I took a job as a facilitator at a government agency. I was teaching life skills and job readiness to ex-offenders and people who were in transition back into the workforce. But it was more than that; it was ministering to them. The encouragement, motivation, and inspiration that I was able to give them through God's words were so powerful that it was like spreading the gospel of Christ to them. And it was acknowledged through the participants' thanks to me about how I helped to change their lives. During graduation, the participants would express how they were impacted by my class instruction and how they now had a new outlook on life, that they had truly been transformed into a changed person.

Don't wait as long as I did. If you obey God's requests, you can develop that personal relationship with Him much faster than me. And truthfully, He really does not have to wait for us. We are supposed to be patient and wait on Him. My grandmother used to say that all the time. "Be patient and wait on the Lord." He will respond and give you what you ask for. But the problem is we are too impatient. We want it right now, not tomorrow or next year, but right now. If God gave it to us right now, most of us could not even handle it. Most of us would be so overwhelmed and excited from His blessings that we would blow it before we had a chance to enjoy it.

Increase Your Faith

Trust and rely on God

Before you begin reading this portion of the book, let's get one thing clear. In order to succeed at anything, you have to have Faith. However, faith without action can be useless. I don't care what your goals or aspirations are in life, without action and faith in God and yourself, it is impossible to achieve any success, goals, or aspirations you have. Success has dangers of its own. When you reach a goal or some prosperity that you have strived for, you may tend to lose faith. This is the time when you should increase your faith because just as you received it, you can also lose it. Many times, spirituality and people's faith can deteriorate.

In his book, Malachi tried to awaken Israel from slacking in relating to God. Years prior, they had optimistically returned to Jerusalem after a long exile. Their faith had grown deeper through difficulties. Despite fierce opposition, they had rebuilt the temple, the symbol of their hope in God. They had expected God to supernaturally fill it with glory and make their nation the center of the world. By Malachi's time, however, Israel's hope had faded. In fact, life seemed to have passed the Israelites by. They could not see that God loved them still and instead they felt that serving God brought no reward.

Have you ever felt as if you had done everything you could do and God still was not answering your prayers? You prayed, you had faith, and still nothing happened? Many Christians think of faith as an almost magical force; if you muster up enough of it, you'll get rich, stay healthy, and live a content life. You may have asked yourself in the past, is it worth the struggle? Faith resembles a difficult race. The runner has his or her eyes on the finish line or prize and, despite nagging temptations to slacken the pace, refuses to let up until he crosses the finish line or gets that prize. That is what you have to do; keep your eyes on the final outcome, despite what challenges that you may face. Remember, God does things on His time, not ours. The key is to be patient and remember that as long as you have faith and work hard it will happen for you.

Back during the days that I served as a police officer, it was considered one of the most dangerous times to be in that position. It was during the early 1990s when crack cocaine had really hit the streets from New York to Washington, D.C., to the West Coast and even southern urban and suburban areas of the country. They were all being saturated with this new and highly addictive drug. And at the time, Washington, D.C., was considered the "murder capital" of the nation. Can you imagine the nation's capital being called the murder capital?

Along with the introduction of crack cocaine to the streets; the increase of various heinous crimes, an increase in robberies and carjacking, and obviously the increase of drug usage by these crack users, or crack heads, as they were deemed. I was never afraid of the crimes or for my life; however, I became more concerned after I was shot at a couple of times.

But what kept me strong and less afraid of the streets as an officer was my faith in God. We had a saying before we left to go out on the streets; it would be better to be judged by 12 than carried by six. What that meant was we would take a chance and explain later to a jury why we shot someone rather than die and be carried to our grave by six pallbearers. Now that may seem like a harsh thing to say, but believe me it helped our psyche on a daily basis. And I always believed that if I was ever shot, I would survive. I believed that because when you feel as if you are doing God's work, you know for sure that you will survive. I was never doubtful that I would be killed on the job.

However, one day on a traffic stop, I was shot at by the driver while I was attempting to write a ticket. The other officers were glad to know that I was not hit, but they kept saying that drug boys could not shoot and that I was lucky. That's not true. First, I don't believe in luck or coincidence. Secondly, it was God that spared my life. And that is what I have always believed. Many people seem to say that they really do have faith, but once they have to face the many challenges of life, their faith becomes questionable.

God created man. He gave us the tools necessary to become whatever we want. I will say it now and will continue to stress it throughout the book – trust and believe that God has already given you the tools needed to succeed. I don't want to offend anyone, so whatever your religion denomination is, remember, I am referencing my God and my own higher belief. Furthermore, it's not important what your religion denomination maybe; just keep in mind that you are not going to make it by yourself. I know, that may be controversial for some, but I am speaking from past experiences, both in life and career. And don't think that for some strange reason you got to where you are today because of some coincidence or luck, because I don't believe in either.

Most people lack the faith to achieve success. I wonder if they lack their faith in God or do they believe in God, but not themselves? Because I believe that the two go hand in hand. If you truly have faith in God, then you surely have to have faith in self, right? Not necessarily. But the real issue that I have is, if God has faith in us and we say we have faith in Him, then why is it that we don't have faith in the self?

It may be that we have become impatient with God. Today, we live life at a much faster pace. Technology has caused us to expect instant gratification. Unfortunately, faith is something that takes time. Just like the blessings of God come when He wants them to, and not when you want them. This is when patience is truly a virtue. And if you really want to achieve the success that you so deserve, you better learn to develop patience. I am not one to criticize anyone because I am working on having more patience and realizing that things are not going to happen when and how I want them to.

In my life, I have been blessed and fortunate enough to experience blessings quickly in some cases, and in other cases, longer than I would have liked. But in either case, God was the determinant in what prevailed. If you don't remember anything else from this book, remember that when you increase your faith and be patient, your success is inevitable. And I believe that even the sky is not the limit!

Because faith is the substance of things hoped for, the evidence of things not seen; you truly have to create a mindset that is programmable by you only – not what tools I use to program myself, but what you do to create the belief that works for you. I find this statement to be one of the most difficult things to try and understand. And my guess for many people is if it does not happen immediately, it won't happen, or if it did not turn out the way they anticipated it, their faith begins to weaken. But without faith, it is impossible to please God – not to mention, please yourself and anyone else.

I know, sometimes it is difficult. But remember this, and you probably have heard it many times, anything worth having is going to be difficult to obtain. And if everyone was going to reach their level of success and dreams, then there would not be anything to hope for. Think back for a second at some other times in your life when things just were not working out for you. Maybe you were having some financial difficulties, relationship or health problems, career or family problems and you could not see any way to solve them or any solution to the problem. What did you do?

I know it all worked out, right? But who worked it out for you? Was it someone who offered you money to help you with that financial setback? Or did a friend really stand by your side and support you when you were having some health problems or coming out of a bad relationship? Whatever the case may have been, you know God was really the one who worked it out for you.

You know that he makes miracles happen, places people in our lives, gives doctors the healing hand to help cure us, and creates opportunities for us that we thought were impossible. And that's having faith, when you really know where the true rewards come from and who really made them happen. And if you are having a difficult time realizing this, you need to increase your faith. Because the more you worry about any given situation or scenario, you are questioning your faith and relationship with God.

Maybe as you are reading this book or have read some success stories about people who have become rich and famous, you are wondering why some people make it to the top and others don't. I will assure you that almost all, if not all, attribute their success to their faith in God. Most of them will share stories about their struggles, their trials and tribulations, and more importantly, how they had to increase their faith and truly believe that one day they would make it. And yes, they had to pay their dues by working hard and having some good connections. But who do you think the connections came from? How do you think they got their big breaks?

My first book, *Overcoming Obstacles...Beating the Odds!* was an autobiographical, motivational, and inspirational self-help book that informed readers how to overcome any obstacle and beat the odds. Regardless of your past life experiences, failures, or past dispositions, I really stressed the importance of maximizing your fullest potential and opportunities.

I was a self-published author trying to get a book deal and doing all the marketing and advertising and promoting by myself. It was very difficult because as a new writer, people have to get to know you. You have to make a good impression in your writing and advertising to get your name out there. Well, I had joined several networking groups as a way to solicit business, sell, and promote my books. One particular networking group had invited me to attend a black tie affair that was honoring *Black Enterprise* magazine's founder and chairman, Earl Graves. Additionally, Academy Award-winning actor Louis Gossett Jr. was going to be the keynote speaker.

The first thing that I thought was, ok, so what, I am going to another function where celebrities would be present – no big deal. After all, I had previously met comedian and radio host Steve Harvey, TV and syndicated radio host Travis Smiley, and hip hop mogul, Russell Simmons – all of whom I had met on at least two separate occasions and given at least two copies of my book. And all of these celebrities worked in the capacity of an event that benefitted children and people in need of life changes.

Ok, so no big deal, I figured they were too busy or did not find the book feasible for what they were doing or were too selfish to help someone out (OK, maybe not). Anyway, I decided to drive to Dulles, Virginia, to the event. The dinner was $150 per person and the drive from my house to the event was about an hour and 15 minutes. Gas prices were just beginning to rise to the ridiculous price of $3.00 a gallon for regular unleaded.

However, it turned out to be a good event and I was able to meet Louis Gossett Jr., who I must add was as inspiring and humble as the true humanitarian that he is. It was an honor and pleasure to have met such an icon. And of course, I asked him would he accept a copy of my book, and he said yes! No big deal at this point. However, he gave me a business card and asked me to call him. Now you know at this point I was astonished! This was the first time that I had met a celebrity and felt like they were interested in my work.

I called and called and left messages for about five months and never had a chance to talk to Mr. Gossett; however, from the time I met him, I felt a connection from God – as if God had actually placed him in my life to help me promote my book. He eventually called me and informed me that he wanted to use by book as a resource tool for his foundation. He also offered to write a forward to the book, to express how he thought the book could help people to overcome obstacles.

Begin with the End in Mind

Once you have truly developed faith in God and self (and only you and God know when that happens), you have to begin your vision with the end in mind. Because many people can't see past tomorrow, never mind the next year or the next five years, it is imperative that you create the best blueprint of where you would like to be. And I always tell people to do it in increments of three to five years. Of course, during that three- to five-year period, there will be many trials, tribulations, and obstacles (that I will discuss later) that are going to be out of your control. But if you begin to envision your dreams, the end is closer than you think.

Begin with the end in mind because you don't know how far and long the journey will be. You must be able to visualize the end. Just as with life, there is a beginning and an ending. Likewise with your dreams; they, too, will have an ending. A large part of how successful you become or whether you reached your goal depends on your outlook. I know…blah, blah, blah, blah. You want to read some magic words or something you never heard before. But guess what? The premise of every success story is based on the vision of that person. It does not matter what your cause is, what product you have to offer, or what skills you possess; all that really matters is how you get to the end. And I believe to get to the end; you have to begin with it in mind.

My story goes way back to early childhood. As a child, I grew up without a father, was sexually abused at age 9, and according to society's standards, I would be dead by the age of 14. Now that was a different era in the world, but the stereotypes and perceptions of people still apply today. Although many youth back then allowed society to dictate their destiny, I never did. I always felt as if I had a chance of becoming successful in life. All I had to do was to program myself to stay focused and stay out of trouble and my situation would only be a temporary mishap, rather than a lifetime failure.

I considered myself different as a child, but not better than most of my peers. I realized that most of my peers could not see past tomorrow. Just like many youth today, they believe that success is a quick fix that happens overnight. And as much as someone preaches to them about it, they still don't get it. It's the same with adults. Most can't see past next week or setting long-term goals to go after a vision or dream.

Even if you had a difficult past, it should not dictate your future. Some critics and educators have said, "Let go of the past." I somewhat disagree. I say, use the past to move forward in life. Use the past as a motivator to know that whatever happens, you are not going back to the way things use to be.

For example, let's say you had drug or alcohol problems in the past. Don't let society dictate that you are likely to relapse in times of trouble and stress for you. Remember earlier when I mentioned the psyche? People allow other's perceptions and stereotypes cause them to develop irrational thinking, ultimately concluding them to believe that there is no hope and that the days of success and dream attainment will never come. In psychology, it has been said that humans only use 10% of the brain, why not try and use all 100%. Do you know how far we all could be if we really used the fullest capacity of the brain?

Here's my point; use the past as a motivator for the future. There is no other way to look at it. Sometimes, I do realize, the past is difficult to let go of depending on the circumstances; however, don't let it dictate who and what you are going to be. Ask yourself this question: Do I really believe that I can achieve my goals and succeed? It is a fundamental question, yet so difficult for people to answer. In many cases, they answer, but are not truthful. You can't fool anyone but yourself. You definitely can't fool God, because He already knows when and if you are going to give up!

Remember this – if you take one step toward going after that dream or goal, I guarantee He will take the next for you. Just ask Him, "God, I need your help. I cannot do this alone. I am afraid, but I really want to go after this dream." The rest will be history. It will happen, no doubt!

If you are reading this book and looking for a magical potion, put it down and never pick it up again. This book is about realization. There are no gimmicks and false pretenses from someone who is here to lie to you. However, if used wisely and read in its entirety, this book can help foster your dreams and goals that you have been procrastinating over. Even if you are already working toward your dreams and goals, there are some critical points here about perseverance, sacrifice, and going through the daunting tasks of ending the journey that can be particularly useful to you.

The key is you have to think BIG! When your visions and dreams are big, you work harder toward them, make unbelievable sacrifices, and can persevere through the daunting tasks that lie ahead. Think small and your results will be small. Remember this: Once you believe in what you can do, all you have left is the hard work! And believe me, the work is hard. But that does not matter. Programming your mind and creating that blueprint is what will separate you from the average person. Remember, in order to be successful, you have to be willing to do things that others won't do.

Don't focus on the here and now, but become a visionary. Always keep your eyes on the prize, even when things seem gloomy and unattainable, because nothing and no one can keep you from achieving your success but you. Remember, God gave you the tools, especially that brain, so use it. Now some might wonder how long they should strive to go after your dreams and goals. I always reply with the one and only authentic answer there could be – until you reach them. Most people get discouraged easily and give up. They may begin with big visions, but once the challenges and struggles begin, they lose insight and can't envision the end.

You may be saying, "But what if…", or "What about…", or "How can I do this or do that when I have to…", and all you are doing is creating excuses to make you lose the vision of the end result. I know, things do happen, but what if I told you that I could promise you that you are never going to die. Would you go after your dreams and goals? Well, guess what? Those are nothing but your psyche's irrational thoughts that can keep you from moving forward. However, you have to be able to rid those thoughts from your mind and program your mind for nothing less than success! And I truly believe that you have what it takes to do just that.

Attitude is everything

Motivational speaker Keith Harrell wrote a book called *Attitude is Everything*. Although I have not read the book, I agree with the title alone with great certainty. Your attitude clearly dictates your outcomes. There is no other way to put it. Because attitude is something that correlates with your personality, it may be difficult to change your attitude. However, if you don't have the right attitude, you will never, ever reach the success or goals that you aspire. Just as faith is the evidence of things not seen, a positive attitude is evidence of things that will be seen. God did not create us to become pessimistic people. He wants us to prosper and live with happiness and success. Unfortunately, the world has interceded and made it difficult at times to continue with a positive attitude. But remember, God is in sole control, no matter what comes your way. He is in control!

A positive attitude is a tough task for many people to develop because attitude has a lot to do with our personality, how we were raised, our family background dynamics, and most importantly, our psyche or cognitive processing. Whenever we attempt to change these things, it is difficult. It is especially difficult when family dynamics and history are involved.

Albert Einstein said it most eloquently that *"the significant problems we face cannot be solved at the same level of thinking we were at when we created them."* With that said, we cannot let the past dictate our future. Whatever problems or bad life experiences that we had up to now MUST be erased. The old attitude of irrational thoughts and shoulda, coulda, woulda obviously got you nowhere. The excuses that were used before now, should not be used again, ever. In fact, with the creation of a new attitude, there are no excuses. The only excuse that the new attitude will create is the excuse to eliminate and not surround you with those unwilling to change their own attitude. Your affirmation should be, *"I don't mind and it doesn't matter."* Simply put, I don't mind that I have a new attitude and it does not matter what you think.

Along with the creation of a new attitude come the naysayers and haters. You know those people who refuse to change their attitude and are mad at you because you have a new one. It's only natural for people to be that way. Remember what I mentioned earlier about how people lack the faith to achieve success? It's the same with their stinking attitude. It's really two-fold – lack of faith and stinking attitude, which lead to failed promises and non-achievers.

Successful people have conquered the challenge of developing the right attitude. For example, the real estate industry was very profitable for both agents and those invested in properties for revenue. But as the economy changed, so did the market and the need for investors and agents became limited. However, the agents and investors who had a positive attitude and patience were able to positively sustain their businesses through the hardships of the real estate market. However, the people who became real estate agents and investors for a quick fix and rapid capital return are the ones who did not last. They went back to their previous jobs before becoming an agent or investor and lost insight of the long-term patience and positive attitude that would have kept them in the game.

No matter what area of life we discuss, the bottom line is a positive attitude is a valuable tool to help you move closer to your dreams and success. I remember growing up and being labeled as a kid that was destined to fail (at least by society's standards), but my positive attitude strengthened my ability to fight those debilitating perceptions that were placed upon not just me but all at-risk youth. They predicted that by the age of 14 or 15, I would either be incarcerated or dead. Today, I am neither. However, I was almost incarcerated and killed (I will cover that later), but my positive attitude prevailed.

Society has a strong influence on our beliefs, our perceptions, and how we want to live our lives. In social psychology, we have concluded that the media has the strongest influence on people. What is said on TV or read in newspapers, magazine articles or on the Internet has greatly influenced people's lives, both positively and negatively. But if you allow society to dictate your chances of becoming successful or fulfilling your dreams, you are truly headed for disaster. The right attitude is what gets you WHAT YOU WANT; the wrong attitude amounts to NOTHING!

I am a prime example of someone who over the years has kept a pretty positive attitude, which may explain how I was able to achieve so much at such a young age. Now, I am not boasting, however, I have been told that I exemplify what it means to display a positive attitude. I have learned to make sure that the affirmations that I create for myself will reveal positive outcomes. For example, when I was a police officer and trying to go back to school, the commanders made it almost impossible for me to go to school and work as an officer. Some of them told me that it was impossible and that there was no way it could be done with my full-time job. Sometimes when people make comments about what you can and cannot do, we tend to embed it in our brains and sometimes really believe them. But because I have always been the type of person that took can't and impossible and turned them into can do and made it possible, I did go to school while working as a police officer.

And that is the motivation that you have to create for yourself. Use the no's and cant's to motivate you to do the opposite. It really can be a useful tool and helpful when people tend to doubt you and not support you. But don't worry, your new attitude is not only more powerful, but it is the crucial key to moving closer to reaching your goals and success!

Spirituality Plays a Major Part, Too

What is spirituality? Spirituality, in a narrow sense, concerns itself with matters of the spirit. The spiritual, involving (as it may) perceived eternal verities regarding humankind's ultimate nature, often contrasts with the temporal, with the material, or with the worldly. A sense of connection forms a central defining characteristic of spirituality — connection to something "greater" than oneself, which includes an emotional experience of religious awe and reverence. Equally importantly, spirituality relates to matters of sanity and psychological health. Like some forms of religion, spirituality often focuses on personal experience.

Spirituality may involve perceiving or wishing to perceive life as more important ("higher"), more complex, or more integrated with one's world view, as contrasted with the merely sensual. Many spiritual traditions, accordingly, share a common spiritual theme – the "path", "work", "practice", or "tradition" of perceiving and internalizing one's "true" nature and relationship to the rest of existence (which can be God, creation, the universe, or life), and of becoming free of the lesser egoist self (or ego) in favor of becoming more fully one's "true self". Today, as you are reading this book and have not figured out what your spiritual connection is, today is that day in which you will begin to seek it. And I know that you have one, otherwise you would not be reading this book.

God is mine. Who's yours? In my opinion, one of the most dangerous people in the world is someone who has no sense of spiritual connection. That is, being able to identify with a higher spirit and connection. You know those people, the ones who think that the world revolves around them and their narcissistic behavior is what has been keeping them from attaining those goals and reaching the level of success they deserve. They think that their hard work, determination, perseverance, and will power is the only way that they were able to live their dreams and reach that desired level of success.

In many instances, I hear people say that they know of a higher power and they are aware that they have a connection with one, but I am referring more to the development of a personal relationship with that higher power. For instance, mine is with God. It took me nearly about 28 years to develop a personal relationship with God. I knew God and believed in him; however, I really did not know Him. When you have that personal relationship with God, it takes time.

As in any relationship, a relationship with God requires time and attention to develop. Your relationship with God will grow for the rest of your life. People have their own special time and place to communicate with God and I am encouraging you to connect to your higher power through prayer or meditation, Bible study, worship, or fellowship.

Prayer or Meditation

Prayer is priceless. It is the most powerful and vital linkage between you and God and creates the bonds of a personal relationship with Him. A family that prays together stays together. It keeps families together, keeps people from losing their sanity, bridges the gap between the believers and non-believers, and gives hope to those in despair. There is no other fundamental premise that accounts for the power of prayer. It means you believe and that by praying you are going to get something in return. I have a saying, "We should stand for something or we'll fall for anything."

Prayer is that practice that you can truly stand for. I have known so many people who never prayed until they were in trouble. We have to learn to pray even when things are going good, too, thanking God for continuously blessing you and your family and letting him know how appreciative you are even though you may have reached your goals and success in life. Although prayer is critical, doing is equally important. You can pray, pray, pray, but God wants you to do something as well. You take the first step; He'll take 10 and lead you to what you are trying to reach. Prayer and doing goes hand in hand; you ask and try and ye shall receive. God wants to see how patient and diligent and faithful you are going to be in the word. Oh, and you can't fool Him. He knows when you pray whether you are authentic or not and where your heart truly is. So don't play games or waste God's time.

If you have not tried it, now is the time. Today, not tomorrow, right now! It is a conversation between you and God that can truly develop that personal relationship that you have been struggling to establish with Him. Through prayer we can praise God for His blessings, repent for our wrongdoings, ask for the needs of our friends and families, and bring our own requests before God. Previously, I mentioned developing a covenant with God; prayer is the first step – that is, asking for that covenant with Him through prayer. It allows us the opportunity to build that personal relationship rather than simply a connection with Him.

"Ask and ye shall receive." My grandma used to say this all the time. Ask God for what you want, be patient and wait on it, have faith and believe that He will give it to you, and sure enough, you will receive it. There is no doubt about it. I am a true testimony of that. Everything that I ever asked God for, HE GAVE IT TO ME! Although it may have taken longer than I would have liked in some cases, He gave it to me. Once you have asked God for it, you don't have to keep asking Him for it. He already knows what you want. I learned that when you keep asking Him over and over again, you are questioning your faith.

Bible Study

There is no other book that is as comprehensive and provides such thorough insight into answering man's concerns and problems than the Bible. Some say the Bible stands for Basic Information before Leaving Earth. Reading and studying the Bible provides insight, explanation, inspiration, and revelation. You do not need a degree or special training to read the Bible. All you need is the desire to know God and learn from Him. Attending bible study also shows your interest, desires, and closer connection to God. Remember, He sees everything, including you going to bible study. So take bible study seriously. If used wisely, it can and will make a difference in your life.

Prayer is not a substitute for reading the word of God. When we pray, we talk to God. And when we read God's word, He talks to us. Of the two, it is more important that God speak to us. First, read the word and then pray. God's word will give us the desire to pray and is a matter for praise and petition when read daily. What we read in the Bible yesterday or a while ago will not give us the spiritual strength we need today any more than the physical food we ate yesterday will give us sufficient bodily strength for today.

Satan hates to have us read the word and does everything he can to block it. Continue to be persistent in taking time to read God's word as Satan is in trying to hinder you and God will help you. Set aside a regular time each day and hold sacred your appointment with God. Ask God to make you hungry for His word. The more you read God's word, the more you will come to love it. Whenever my grandmother had a crisis, she would always read the Bible then pray. She would recite verses to us and then say that she would leave it up to God to take care of her problems. If more of us would decide to pray before we made hasty decisions, a lot more people would have peace in their lives.

Worship and Fellowship

"Be completely humble and gentle; be patient, bearing with one another in love. Make every effort to keep the unity of the Spirit through the bond of peace."
Ephesians 4:2-3 (NIV)

Fellowship is a relationship of inner unity (collectivism) among believers that expresses itself in outer co-participation with Christ and one another in accomplishing God's work on earth. Fellowship is God's way of accomplishing His plan of glorifying Christ. It is the indispensable means of accomplishing the God-given purpose of the church. Fellowship is communion with other believers in order to encourage each other's walk with the Lord. It is the love of Christ that can unite people from diverse backgrounds and with distinctive personalities so that they are able to call each other "brother" and "sister."

The word fellowship in the New Testament is translated from the Greek word, "koinonia". This word means an association, community, communion, joint participation, or intercourse. It means sharing with other people. To be involved in Christian fellowship with others means to share your life with others. We share our lives with others and also with Christ, who promises to be with us when two or three are gathered together in His name (Matthew 18:20). Fellowship with Christ and other believers involves feeding on the Word together. Sometimes it means eating meals together (Acts 2:46).

In fellowship, we share our time, gifts, and talents, both spiritual and natural. We also share our money as God leads, and according to the needs of the group (2 Corinthians 9). This does not mean that Christians should **expect** other Christians to support their families. Be very cautious about each other's expectations especially in regards to money. It has and can be our worst enemy.

Read 1 Timothy 5:8. Christians are commanded to work diligently and honestly so that they have something to share with those in need (Ephesians 4:28). Christian fellowship exists not only to meet the needs of Christians emotionally, socially, mentally, spiritually, and where necessary, financially. It also exists to demonstrate to the world the meaning of Christian love and to call people out of the world into that fellowship with Christ and His body. In fellowship with Christ and with one another, we are coming not only to receive but also to give. This is where our dedication to Christ's Lordship will be made practical, and hence, proved real.

Get in a good Bible-based church. Worshiping and gathering with other Christians is vital to growth and accountability in a Christian life. By doing this, you can learn from others. You will share commonalities and help each other. The same premise applies to people in transition to changing their lives; you have to surround yourself with people that are on the page as you. It makes no sense whatsoever to be in the presence of people that are doing the total opposite of you. They will only bring you down, distort your thinking, and demolish your dreams. Here are some spiritual tips for entering seriously into committed relationships with real Christians (those who are trustworthy in Christ and want to refrain from sin).

1. <u>The people you choose to associate with can affect your destiny.</u> It's like anything else that we do in life. Those that surround themselves with people of similar interests are more likely to be more committed and dedicated to the cause of serving. Likewise, do not be deceived – evil company corrupts good habits (morals).

2. <u>God has planned for you to receive love and encouragement from His family on earth.</u> True Christians have your back. They go far and beyond the expectations of the so-called fair-weathered friends. They will be there to encourage you in times of trouble and will always be a shoulder for you to weep on.

3. <u>God wants you to learn to give love and encouragement to your brothers and sisters in Christ.</u> Stop bringing each other down. Encouragement is a must. God placed specific people in our lives for a purpose. Don't allow the negative energy of a gossiper to destroy your ability to help save someone.

4. <u>You can learn wisdom from more mature Christians by being with them.</u> It's like having a mentor – something that everyone needs. "He who walks with wise men will be wise" If you are the smartest person among the company of Christians you are with, it may be time to change company. You never want to be the smartest person among your group; how can you grow and mature as a Christian this way?

5. <u>You can be built up in faith by hearing the preaching of anointed ministers of Christ.</u> "Faith comes by hearing" (*Romans 10:17*). The preaching of the word should build up your faith and confidence in the promises of God.

6. <u>If you remain in a church where the people don't listen to the word of God and obey it (Deuteronomy 28), their example and their teaching will lead you to hell.</u> Be aware of false prophets and those who display a portrayal of being anointed in the word.

7. <u>God wants you to serve Him effectively. You can't do it without cooperating with other Christians.</u> Be careful about talking too much! The more you talk, the less you listen, and the less you listen, the less you hear, which ultimately affects your understanding of the word and mission in serving God.

8. <u>When you repent and receive Christ by faith as Lord, you are summoned into the body of Christ. You have a part to play in Christ's body.</u> We have an obligation to use our God-given talents and abilities to help others (*1Corinthians 12:12-28*).

9. <u>You cannot fulfill the commands of Christ and of the apostles without entering into fellowship.</u> How can you love one another, encourage one another, admonish or counsel one another, serve one another, if you are never with "one another"?

10. <u>God commands you to come to attend church gatherings regularly.</u> How can you help others that are following Christ if you are not attending church? Remember, being a mentor means role modeling for others and having a presence in others' lives, so go to church!

Plant an Abundant Spiritual Harvest

Life is a cooperative effort between God and man – giving someone else an opportunity, a chance to pick themselves up after a setback, a failure or life-changing event. Don't forget how we were when we needed help and, for most of us, the help you thought you had did not really help out at all. Every time you are willing and able to help someone and you do, it brings you to a closer relationship with God. What did He do? He ministered to the poor, healed the sick, and helped those that were unable to help themselves. When you are more fortunate than someone else, we are supposed to help them. I know, you say, but I tried to help them but they won't change or it has not helped them. I say, as long as you make a conscious effort to help them and in the process, do your best, the rest will eventually fall into place.

Like everything that happens in life, good or bad, it too shall pass that that person you planted a seed for is now soaring into the person they set out to be. He or she will now reap the benefits of being that positive person or getting the desired rewards out of life, too. Sometimes the notion of helping someone is like faith. You either have it in you or you don't. Don't always look for rewards when you help someone; God sees it and you are being rewarded, whether you know or not.

Act 2

> "It's not the ideas we don't have that prevents us from being creative…it's the ideas that imprison our thinking."
>
> -Roger von Oech

Who are you?
Create Your Personal Picture

First of all, if you don't already know, you are a child of the highest God. You are a champion in the making, a conqueror, a victor, and a person that God created for greatness. You have the ability to become everything that you aspire to be. Your abilities are infinite. And life is clearly what you make it to be. No one and nothing shall stop you from reaching your goals in life. God created these premises for you early on in life.

But I want to go back even further and ask you, does life begin at conception or at birth? When does the creation of personal self begin? God's love and involvement with our lives starts long before our birth – who we will become, what type of image we will hold for ourselves and what our full potential in life will be. A famous psychologist by the name of Erik Eriksson developed an assessment to explain how we grow as humans from birth to late adulthood. It explains in great detail how we create a picture of ourselves based on our environment and the people closest to us.

Adolescent Identity vs. Role Confusion

This is probably the most critical stage of identifying who we are. It is probably the most difficult to understand both from the adolescent standpoint and as parents. The adolescent tries to integrate many roles (child, sibling, student, athlete, and worker) into a self-image while being influenced by role models and peer pressure. I won't discuss all of Eriksson's stages, but the one that appears to be more logical for identifying who I am would be the fifth developmental stage, wherein adolescents begin to seek their true identity. The adolescent must make a conscious search for identity. This is built on the outcome and resolution of conflict from earlier stages. If the adolescent cannot make deliberate decisions and choices, especially about vocation, sexual orientation, and life in general, role confusion becomes a threat. The central question of this stage is, of course, "Who am I?"

Eriksson concluded that, "Teens need to develop a sense of self and personal identity." Success leads to an ability to stay true to you, while failure leads to role confusion and a weak sense of self. Just as many people go through life resistant to change, likewise the inability to answer the question, "Who am I?" is equally vital for continuous personal and career growth in life. Are you able to answer this question and know what you are capable of accomplishing in life? If not, don't worry; help is on the way.

It will take some work, but you have to do some sacrificing. You have to sacrifice something to be able to attain something else. Simply put it, get ready to identify things about you that may cause anxiety and fearful feelings to surface. The self is such a critical component to look at. Some of you may already be heading in the right direction of doing this, but others may still need some help. Look at the following scenario and place yourself in the shoes of John.

According to society, John should be financially and emotionally stable; instead, he has suffered from several financial setbacks and goes around with a very cynical and self-defeating attitude. But John is no different from other people who go through similar and worse setbacks, except for one thing – he let it take control of his life to a point that he has never reached the level of success he desired. And if you ever talk to him, within the first five or 10 minutes, you can tell why. His pessimistic, cynical outlook on life is awful; everybody else is always less than he. Rarely is credit given to anyone for any purpose whatsoever. He has a problem with holding himself accountable for the shortcomings and failures in his life. He ridicules and badgers others rather than exhibiting his God-given altruistic behaviors.

This is a very ironic and unusual characteristic for a man as educated and experienced in life as John. However, something is terribly wrong. In most people's eyes, John would be considered smart and financially well off. He holds several terminal degrees, yet he is always complaining about money and exudes negativity. John is one of those people who can find fault in Jesus Christ! And anyone that can find fault in Jesus has to be cynical. John, like many others, had his share of setbacks, challenges and obstacles to overcome; however, his mind is full of what I like to call *"imprisoned thinking"* – that is, most his negative experiences have been created by the ideas manifested in his mind.

Some of those ideas are created by society's false perceptions about who we are based on our past, while others have been verbally said to and taught to us by family, friends, or others who claim to have our best interests at heart. By now you are probably aware that we create most of the faulty things about ourselves even before society begins to create them. The more negative images that are created; the more we tend to believe those thoughts. And this can be detrimental to those suffering from low self-esteem or those who have been victims of various types of abuse.

Part of the reason why John has not progressed during his life is due to his inability to paint a vivid personal picture of the self – that is, being able to identify who John truly is, which ultimately will help further his potentials in life. Yes, he is highly educated, but just because you have several degrees does not mean that you are smart or financially secure.

Intelligence has nothing to do with this scenario of John. John, like many educated people, waits for handouts and opportunities that others will give him instead of creating his destiny. Nobody is going to just give you anything. It was once said by the late, great Nannie Helen Burroughs *"that man has to stop asking God to do for them what he can do for self."* Sometimes you may get some help, but ultimately they will want something in return. Even when you ask God for something, you still have to put in some work and effort. In fact, when you take one step, He will help you complete the steps that follow.

I don't care how smart you are or think you are, what's impressive to me is desire and action. John is clearly one of those people that can steal your dream. Literally, talking to John is like talking to most non-believers – a waste of time. Most importantly, how well you see yourself through your own evaluation and abilities is critical, not what some degree or title has given you. And you know that is what many people look at – what degree you have or what school you attended, all of which are irrelevant.

Remember this – the most successful and wealthiest people are not even college graduates. They are people who were able to identify who they were and what their potential was and they went after it. That is, they hustled their way to success. They truly believed that their dream was attainable. They closely looked at the self and realized that what most people don't have, they did. They had the ability to achieve greatness! And that is what you have to do. No matter what circumstances arise, the self is the most powerful evaluation to help you reach your success!

For a moment I want you to forget about how smart you are or how much money you would like and ask yourself this question: Am I willing to do whatever it is to gain my success or achieve my goals? Remember this, you are going to program your mind for nothing less than attaining that success or dream. And that means going far and beyond what most people are willing to do. In order to become successful; you have to be willing to do what others will not do. It is a basic rule. It does not matter how much money you have or how smart you are. When it all comes down to it, the evaluation of the self is the pivotal point for programming your mind for any successful endeavor.

One of the critical elements in the evaluation of self is the creation of *positive thinking*. Unfortunately in life, we tend to make decisions based on what has happened in the past, not what we want in the future. And that alone debilitates the logical and rational thinking and pessimistic attitude about self, others, and the world in general. And once we close in on that belief, then we close out all other possibilities to create the positive self.

Since the world is surrounded by negativity, doubtful thoughts, non-believers, and complacency, you have to be able to embed in your mind that nothing will stop you from achieving the success you deserve. Easier said than done? Why – because in the past you have read books on how to program your mind and you started but did not finish? Or you thought the book was too critical and complicated to follow, or was it that the book was directly talking about you and you got offended? Whatever the case may have been, take this time to begin evaluating you.

I was speaking to a group of people and during the speaking engagement I mentioned that the self is the most difficult to evaluate. The crowd went bizarre! It was like I had told them that I was giving them some money. They yelled and screamed, "You're right", "That's right". They kept saying, "Say it again, brother; say it again." I thought to myself, I am truly onto something here. But what I realized was that the word "self" can be such a frightening word.

When you ask someone to take a closer look at the self, you are asking them to find the faults, weaknesses, fears, excuses, and all the reasons they have not made it. And in many cases, the fault is almost always someone else. There are not too many times, initially at least, that people really take a closer look at the self and say, "You know what, I really do need to work on something." That's the hard part. The easy part is to blame someone else for your discrepancies and mishaps in life. But I always tell people if you point your finger at someone, you have three other fingers that are pointing right back at you. Try it now and you will see exactly what I am talking about. Now, three surely outweighs one, right?

Who is a better evaluator of the self than you? The evaluation of the self can work in two distinct ways; first, you are the *best* evaluator of *you*. No one can tell you what you are capable of doing, well maybe they can, but it does not matter. You are truly the one who knows your strengths, weaknesses, and more importantly, what you are willing to sacrifice. Secondly, the evaluation of the self can be detrimental. It can cause us to become cynical, too critical of the self, and can create irrational instead of rational thinking. But don't worry, you will not allow this to happen. Instead, you will focus on what is best for you and the best route to take to get there.

The one that has really helped me throughout my life and career is the ability to program myself for success. For those of you who have read my first book, *Overcoming Obstacles...Beating the Odds!*, one of the things that I talked about very often throughout the book was my ability to create opportunities based on the ability of me to program my mind for any endeavor that I pursued. And through the blessings of God and support of family, the tasks that lied ahead to reach my goals became easier and easier.

I have a saying, "If you want it, go get it." You may be saying, yeah right, that sounds easy. But the fact of the matter is that when you want something so badly, it really does become easy. OK, maybe easy is not the word that you want to hear. Maybe you want to hear more attainable. Whatever word you like, the only thing that matters is you have the power to make the decision and program yourself to go after what it is that you want. And if you want it bad enough, you will do what it takes to get there.

You should be dreaming the dreams and practicing your accomplishments as if you already have attained them. I know you are worried about what people will think of you. Let's get something straight right now; people should be the least of your worries! Most people don't want to see you make it anyway. Remember, these are probably the people who did not have the courage or strength to take on their own dreams and aspirations. Misery loves company! And non-believers don't believe in themselves, so why do you think they will believe in you?

The best is yet to come

As I mentioned earlier, Erik Eriksson's' research concluded that evaluation of the self really begins early in life. During the early childhood years, children really begin to explore, understand, and evaluate who they are and what they are capable of. Although when we discuss the personality, educators have concluded that the personality is fully developed between the ages of five and six. After that, your personality is the way you will be for the rest of your life. And psychologists say that the only way your personality can change is through some traumatic event, a religious change, or some major life changing event; however, there is not enough definitive evidence to conclude these findings one way or the other.

If you can remember back as a child, especially during your early childhood years, those years tend to have been the most memorable for you. Those were the years when you solely relied upon others to care for you. You were mostly dependent on someone to do something for you. I remember my early childhood days like they were yesterday. And although my experience during the early years of my life were mostly traumatic, God kept a protective shield over me and allowed me to live through even the most daunting and troublesome times in my life. It was not until later on as an adult that I realized He was preparing me to serve others in need of help. And I thank Him for that. I discovered early in life that I was going to care for others. I always had a keen interest in helping others. It has been my nature for as long as I can remember and I am glad because today it has grown to become my passion. And when you have a passion for something, it becomes second nature. You become great at it and enjoy it at the same time!

As a teen, we were really concerned with our looks. And for some of us, those hormonal changes including acne, voice changes, and rapid growth spurts that all could have been, at times, frightening. But the bottom line was our appearance. We really cared what others thought about us. And I think today it is equally important to us as adults; although most of us admit that we don't care what others think of us, I believe otherwise. And that is how society has us thinking, concerned with what others think or have said about us. How long do we continue to live our lives based on the perceptions of others? People are going to talk about you regardless.

My point is this – taking a closer look at the self has always been an integral part of our growth as a person. Throughout our childhood to our adulthood, the only way to reach any level of success is to understand the self. And yes, we all have weaknesses as well as strengths that have either caused us to fail or allowed us to succeed. But by evaluating the self, we can begin to use the past failures, mishaps, and difficulties of life experiences to overcome all the challenges and obstacles that come our way.

The next time that you are in front of a mirror, do a quick evaluation of the *self*. Ask yourself some questions, but be ready to answer them truthfully or else you will be lying to yourself. Here are five critical questions you should be asking yourself. Of course, the answers will vary depending on the individuality of each person; however, they are universal questions. They are as follows:

1. *Who am I?*

    First and foremost, this question can really relate to a number of situations from family to work to relationships to friends. Once again, when answering this it is important to realize that we are now in a situation where the truth will be able to set us free. And I pose this question first because the person not knowing the self is the same person with no direction headed for nothing.

2. *What is my purpose?*

    Some people go a lifetime and never realize what their purpose is. Remember this – God gave us all distinct talents and abilities. Most of us do not capitalize on the God-given talents that we possess. Instead, we go around confused, blame others for our failures, and never reach our fullest potentials in life. If you don't know what your purpose is in life, I suggest you talk to God and ask Him. He will guide you in the direction where your talents and abilities are most useful.

3. *Will I stop blaming others for my failures and shortcomings in life?*

Blah, blah, blah, and the promises continue to dwindle into nothing. I know it's not you, but your brother, mother, spouse, mentor, teacher and everybody else that you can put the blame on. You know that you have made this promise to yourself so many times that you have lost count. But ask yourself, are you really willing, ready, and serious about making the necessary sacrifices to go after what you really deserve?

4. *Am I willing to make the necessary sacrifices to go after my dreams and the success I deserve?*

I know it's tough to make the financial and emotional setbacks that come with sacrifices. Maybe that expensive, beautiful car or that big house and large mortgage payment have to be cut back so you are able to invest in self in order to get to the end of that journey. And ask yourself, do I really want to give up these small material things to get the larger payoff later on? Most people make sacrifices that are superficial. That is, until the real sacrifices are to be made, their decision to go after their dreams becomes less desirable and meaningful than before.

5. *Do I have what it takes to make it happen?*

God said you do, so why do you continuously question yourself about your ability to persevere through the daunting tasks of gaining your success and reaching your dreams? You are the only person that can truly answer this question for yourself. In the past, obstacles, challenges, distractions, and even circumstances prohibited you from reaching the top, right? Bologna! These past things that occurred are just the things that happen in everyone's life; you just let them take advantage of you and that kept you from moving forward!

When answering these questions, it is important to realize that no matter what your answers may be, opportunities, dreams, and success are only a step away. It all depends on how bad you want it. God already knows the end point, so all we can do is enjoy the journey, pray, and hope for the best. Your best is clearly yet to come. But you won't know your best outcome if you don't put in your best effort. Remember this – you get back what you put in. If you work hard, make the necessary sacrifices, and be patient, God will surely reward you.

It's Not Where You Started, but Where You Finished

The evaluation of the self can often elicit uneventful life experiences, past traumatic events, and things that we really want to delete from our recollections of life. Let's say, for example, that you had a very traumatic childhood experience. You experienced physical, sexual, or verbal abuse or neglect in some fashion. By society's standards, you were labeled as destined for failure. But looking back on those early days of your life and comparing it to where you are today, you can distinctively see how your life is totally different than it could have been.

At least that is how it turned out for me. I was sexually abused at an early age, fatherless, and considered poor. But through the grace of God and evaluation of my own self, as well as capitalizing off my abilities and God-given talents, I was able to rid myself of the negativity and became somebody, instead of society's nobody. Even if you did not experience a traumatic childhood or life experience, at some point in your life, you began something, but for some reason or another did not finish. You know those excuses that I discussed earlier as to why you have not achieved your success or reached your goals or dreams. Today, those excuses are going out the window forever. Whatever you started, you have to finish. Even if at times it seems as if it is not going to happen for you, you must keep reaching for it!

History teaches us that the most successful people had the most difficult times in their lives. That is because nothing worth having is going to be easy. The obstacles and challenges that will come your way may seem unbearable at times, but I can truly say and I believe that there is no obstacle or challenge that can't be conquered. Put your faith in God and your willingness and self-determination is all you need. If it was so easy, then everyone would reach their level of success and be financially well off. Whatever start you had, don't allow it to dictate your destiny. If you let the beginning of some bad starts ruin your life, then you have failed no one but yourself.

As previously discussed, we have already decided not to blame anyone anymore for our lack of success and failures in life, right? So the same principle will apply to the beginning and the ending of your journey. It's not where you start, but where you finish. So ask yourself, am I going to finish?

The Past Should Not Dictate Your Future

So what life has not been fair? You think God has to give you an explanation as to why life can be so difficult? If so, you're wrong. He is the power of all power and owes nobody answers. And I agree with you, life can and will be a challenge.

The past can come back in other forms as well, such as having been in a bad marriage and now being afraid to ever get married again. Telling your children about some of the things you did in your younger days to stop them from making the same mistakes, only to find out that they did them anyway because "you did it." Then there is the good side of how your past will dictate your future. Your children have all grown up and you decide to return to school to get the college degree you never got when you were younger because you were too busy raising a family.

Ultimately, we really should be focusing on using the past as a means of not making the same mistakes again. Some of us had a rough upbringing and refused to allow what society said about us and how we were destined for failure to come true. I have always used myself as an example of someone who truly beat the odds that were totally against me. Once I realized that God had great things for me, I then realized I could do anything in life because God had my back. Everything began to fall into place.

Many people today still use the past as an alibi for not being productive and reach their goals or success in life. They feel that since they came from a dysfunctional family (i.e., drugs, abuse, and other unfortunate life instances), it will always come back to haunt them. I am here to tell you that whatever happened in the past, you should not allow it to dictate your future. You can use the past only if it is going to be beneficial in moving forward with what you want in life. I know, we may never be able to forget the past, but the sooner you forgive those who hurt you, the better off you will be for the future. Once you forgive people and situations in life, you can better deal with future setbacks, challenges, and obstacles that come your way. And, you can help others with their situations, too. Put God first in everything that you do and you will not be sorry – in your decisions that you make with your spouse, your family, your children, and even your finances.

You've heard people say don't look at the past, just focus on the future. That is a good saying; however, the past can be an invaluable reminder of where we don't want to be. You can use the past to strengthen your will power and determination to attain your goals and dreams. Many people get caught up in the past so much that it becomes like the irrational thoughts and ideas that ruin our psyche; it dooms them for failure. Indeed, dwelling on the past too much can have you going right backward rather than forward.

In fact, you should begin affirming to yourself that your past will and cannot dictate your future. You should embed this in your brain and remind yourself from time to time when things get rough and looming. If you will do these small, remote things, I guarantee that your life will change. Remember that the best is always yet to come if you believe that God has your back. No one will ever be able to mistreat you or make you feel unwanted or ruin your self-image ever again when you walk with Jesus.

The Vitality of Your Personal Picture

Have you ever wondered why you can't see yourself reaching certain heights or achieving certain goals in life? What have you done in the past that has prohibited you from seeing your future? Have thoughts of others caused you to create an image of yourself that is truly not you? If you have answered yes to any of these questions, I suggest you read this next section. Create a personal picture for yourself. That is, create a self-image and concept of who you want to be. In the past, you may have based your self-image and self-concept on what others have said or done to you rather than what God's word has been for you. Regardless of how much money you have or what kind of house you live in, how you paint that personal picture of yourself will have a tremendous impact on how far you will go. And the truth of the matter is, if you paint a bleak, unclear, distorted picture of you then that is just what your image will be. On the contrary, if you are able to create a clear, concise, and vivid personal picture, your image and actions will become clearer, ultimately allowing you to understand who you are and what direction you are moving in.

Your personal picture should become so vivid that you can almost feel it. You know how you have been so close to achieving something and all of a sudden something happened and you never go it? It's the same with the creation of your personal picture. Once you have created it, nothing can take it away. You are being truthful to yourself, something that many people are afraid to do.

Your picture has to have meaning to it, otherwise it becomes useless. People usually won't take you seriously if your personal picture has no substance or meaning to it. I say your actions will speak louder than your words; they always do. Because the picture that you paint in the eyes of others should be the same picture that you paint behind closed doors. By doing this, you reduce the chances of being a hypocrite. No one believes you when you are a hypocrite.

Often at times, our personal picture can and will change. When life takes us through trials and tribulations, we often change the way we see ourselves, our abilities and our personal pictures. That can be bad and good. It can be used as motivation or debilitation. But you can better control that if you see the situation as God sees it – that you are strong and courageous, and a man or woman of great courage, determination, will power, and the ability to overcome any obstacle or challenge. Start painting your personal picture as God sees you. That is, quit making excuses about what you should have done and begin to step out on faith and do what God has for you to do. You are a child of the highest God and you are to settle for nothing less.

Think back for a moment to a situation when you painted a negative picture for yourself and it prohibited you from excelling at something that you truly wanted and deserved. You made the decision not to take a leadership position at work because in the past it was at times stressful, brought you out of your comfort zone, and required you to do something different. And the truth of the matter is; you did not do it because you focused on *if* instead of *I can*. This happens to too many of us who have created this distorted personal picture of ourselves. It has led us into accepting less than we want and deserve in life. Our relationships with people have suffered, our financial means, our careers, and our relationship with God has been limited. We have allowed so many factors to affect our ability that it is frightening.

But I am writing to you today to let you know that you are an exceptional person. When God created you, He created an exception to the rule. And that is exactly the picture that you have to paint. I was watching T.D. Jakes on TV and he mentioned the fact that exceptional people have exceptional challenges. I truly agreed with him. The more exceptional you are, the more difficult the trials and tribulations are. That's because what you see yourself as is likely the person that you will be. If every time you experience challenges and setbacks in life and you allow them to overrule your ability to recover and comeback, you are showing God that you are not that exceptional person that He has made you to be. As you already know the more difficult the tribulation, the greater the outcome.

Understand that you are not here by chance, that God brought you here for a purpose. He gave us all the mind and ability to create an image that would be positive and full of purpose. However, society has influenced us with false self-images of what people think we should be rather than the people that we actually are. Learn to guard and control your personal picture of yourself so that no one is able to distort it.

Be careful about sharing your personal picture with others. They may appear to be happy for you, but instead, they may be the same people that will try to destroy it. God wants you to use that positive personal picture to motivate yourself to do whatever you want in life. Stop using the same old excuses time after time that have stopped you from moving ahead in life. Now is the time to create that personal picture that you have always dreamed of. It's not as difficult as it seems; you just have to take the first step and have faith and the rest will come.

"WHAT CONCERNS ME IS NOT THE WAY THINGS ARE, BUT RATHER THE WAY PEOPLE THINK THINGS ARE."

-Epictetus

Act 3

Identify Your Challenges and Barriers to Change

Ask yourself, what is it that is keeping me from making the changes in my life that I know I need to make? If you are like a lot of people, then fear, leaving your comfort zone, anxiety, lack of hope, faith and taking risks are all common for those who have not made a conscious effort to tackle the challenges and overcome the barriers that have been holding you back for years. And when we look at those challenges and barriers, we realize that they are not as bad as it seems; in fact, nothing is ever as bad as it seems.

We tend to make situations worse than they really are, most of the time by the self-pity and disparities that we hold about self and the perceptions that society holds about us. My challenge to you is to ask yourself, what habits do you have that are barriers to what you want in life?

When we set visions or goals, we are intentionally creating stress and tension between where we are now, or current reality, and where we want to be – the vision. Usually, this stress and tension creates the drive and motivation to go after our dreams and reach our goals. Unfortunately, the setbacks, obstacles and challenges contribute to us taking the easy way out and the path of least resistance. And this is when people give up. They think that because they experienced some setbacks and challenges in life that it's impossible to change. The self-talk (which we will discuss later) takes over their thought process. They begin to say things like, "I wish, I think, maybe, and if." These are doubtful words that question your vision, reality and ability to move forward after those major setbacks and life's challenges.

You probably have a few barriers and challenges that are standing in your way and keeping you from challenging yourself to new levels of greatness. Barriers, though they are sometimes self-talked-up obstacles, seem very real at the moment you experience them. What you must realize is that whenever you find yourself resisting anything during the process of change, it is fear talking to you.

Once you begin to understand why you're having difficulty moving forward in the process of change, you can identify the fear and be ready to move on with confidence and embrace your greatness. Identify your barriers and then you can begin to come up with a plan so that you can take action and let the momentum you create help carry you towards the life you want and deserve. The following are a few common barriers and challenges that people face during their act of change:

1. Time - I hear this one all the time. And yes, I am calling it an excuse because that is exactly what it is. First and foremost, God wants us to serve and help others, but we can't help anyone until we help ourselves first. We must take time for ourselves! Remember this – we are making changes for us, not everyone else, so I am first. However; it's difficult to commit time, especially when you are working a full-time job. We're taught to serve others' needs and wants before our own and often wind up tired, overscheduled and with no energy for ourselves. You should schedule daily and weekly appointments with yourself in order to take time away from your busy life and become clear on where to direct your energy and time.

2. Fear of change and success - As John 14:1-4 said, "Do not be fearful; Do not let your hearts be troubled; trust also in me." Surprisingly, after all these words from God and all the sacrificing that some people make to reach a certain level of success, some are still afraid of success! It requires more

responsibility and you are expected to do better than others. Many people enjoy the titles and prestige they hold and don't want to make a change to become more successful. Therefore, they become stagnate and refuse to grow any further. Though they state that they do, indeed, want more success, they choose to stay in their comfort zone. Success is the unknown and the unknown is often feared. Increased success means change and an increased level of responsibility.

It takes courage and risk for most of us to take the leap and find a fulfilling job. After we've achieved success, we must maintain that success and that takes effort. We must live with a new sense of self and change a new view of ourselves and a new way of relating to the world. It is so much easier to daydream about "someday" than it is to actually take the steps to make "someday" a reality and live it on a day-to-day basis. That requires work and commitment and many of us find it easier to live in a fantasy of "shouda, coulda, woulda, if..."

3. Fear of failure – This is the most common fear of them all. We fear so many things about failure. We fear the fear of failure. In other words, we fail ourselves even before we give ourselves a chance to succeed or fail. We fear losing our stability (money), we fear falling down, we fear making the wrong choices, we fear not being able to live up to standards (whether they are ours or society's), and the biggest fear is that of which we fear being labeled a failure or a loser. There are so many other fears, it's almost erratic.

4. Loneliness and lack of support - Loneliness can be a dream job killer. We all need moral and financial support in times of change. Confidence in ourselves and the ability to move forward are often conglomerates when we have a great support system. When we find ourselves trying to go it alone, it's more likely that the setbacks, challenges and obstacles are much more difficult, ultimately taking us further back than before. In many cases, understanding who you are and what you enjoy doing is enhanced with the help of others. If we lack the support, many

times it's too overwhelming and can be discouraging, ultimately dampening our chances to make those changes in our lives.

5. <u>Promises made by family and society</u> - Throughout our lives, we hear many messages about how we should act. We become conditioned and socialized to act in acceptable ways that may not always be in our best interests. We often live a life doing what others tell us we should. We're told/taught, "Don't rock the boat," "Fit in, be like everyone else," "This is how it's done" and more. Being like everyone else may not be where our greatness lies and we wind up not even knowing what we want in a dream job. We fear rejection so much that we often play small just to fit in. We take our place as one of the mindless worker ants, trudging through the same routines, complaining about the same problems, and realizing the same small results. We must move from our "should" to our genuine wants or desires.

6. <u>Financial obligations and fear of poverty</u> - People say all the time, "How am I going to pay my bills, how am I going to feed the family? I have one solution to this question: Matthew 6:25-34. Don't worry about food, clothes or your body; each day has its own troubles of its own. If your survival depends on your income alone, this is a fear you may experience when facing dramatic changes in your life. Recognize that you have control over the changes you wish to bring about and can do so gradually while maintaining a secure income from a familiar source. Thus, you can ease into the life you want one step at a time and reduce the threat of poverty.

7. <u>Comparing and despairing</u> - 2 Corinthians 10:12 said, "For we dare not make ourselves of the number, or compare ourselves with some that commend themselves: but they measuring themselves by themselves, and comparing themselves among themselves, are not wise." Comparison is a losing game. It lets us run round in endless circles and provides many excuses for not doing anything more. For

example, you say something like, "I'll never be as good a pastor as so and so. I'll never have a church with 20,000 members."

8. Self-doubt - James 2: 14-19 said, "We see ourselves as less than who we really are and feel we are unworthy to receive all that we deserve. Our own fears, limitations and mental criticisms alienate us from our goal. Self-doubt is one of the biggest obstacles to achieving our dreams. We often ignore ourselves in favor of others. We value their opinions too highly and our own too little. The only real approval that matters is that which comes from inside us. We're the only people who know what we truly need and want. This makes us our own best judge of whether or not what we're doing is right and good for us. We must shift from self doubt to belief. If we tap into our true gifts and unleash our essence, we come from a place of strength. It is possible to be all we can during the dream job process.

9. Not sure what you would love to do- Many people don't know what they want or what they enjoy doing. They limit their potential because they do not explore opportunities. In many instances, they block opportunities rather than capitalizing on them. They aren't sure where they are going and how to get there. This frustration of not knowing can cause people from taking the risk and having the courage to find out what they would love to do.

10. Fear of making the wrong decision- (Exodus 3:11) Moses had big doubts about his ability to lead. He resisted God, bringing up his unworthiness and lacks of authority his fear of people's distrust. Every decision you have to make can lead you down a daunting path with challenges and opportunities of its own. You may have several options you would like to try and worry that only one will be the right one and spend endless time trying to decide which is best. Carefully thinking a situation through in a thorough manner is a good thing.

We should begin to ask God first, then weigh the advantages and disadvantages and make a conscious decision to choose the best way to achieve our goals. However, analyzing can be used to avoid action. We can make endless lists, but if items never get checked off the list, what good is it? It's easy to get lost in the details and never get around to doing anything because you're too busy planning for every possible contingency. Life is as difficult as you make it. And for God's sake can we stop saying "life is too short"? It is not so easily placed into right or wrong, good or bad. However, there will always be various areas of gray. Resist the thinking of fear and decide that it's nothing more than a mere case of the enemy trying to hold you back.

We must build a vision that incorporates the word of God and seek out what plans HE has for us. Once that plan is put into place, it will overrule the current situation or reality that may impact our decision to go back to the current reality. In the process identifying those barriers and challenges to change, we must remove all the excuses and negativity from our minds even if the current reality is far worse than the vision. We have to learn to avoid patterns of self-pity and irrational thoughts that serve as barriers to change. Here are some tips to avoid doing when you are challenged and barriers are in your way;

1. **<u>Never give up of the vision, stay focused.</u>** If you can't see past tomorrow, you can forget it. You have to be able to see beyond your current situation to begin tackling the issue. This is one of the first things we tend to do. We lose insight and direction of our vision. The setback was so detrimental that we lost our focus and vision. Under no circumstances, should you ever lose insight of your vision or focus. It can and will ruin your aspirations, hopes and definitely your dream. Develop a plan B. Most of the time, we have not thought about a plan B. Its' good to have one because it prepares us to continue on after setbacks and failures in life. Never get caught without a plan B, you may never regain that focus or vision.

2. **Focus on the Solution, not the problem.** Here is where many people fall short. They dwell so much on what has happened that they don't allow themselves to create solutions. The problem has become so overwhelming that it overrides most of your God-give problem solving skills. Don't focus on your current situation so much that it creates more stress. You may have a drinking or drug problem, but going to meetings and on your way to recovery. You may have just lost your job, but you have several interviews and some strong prospects ahead. In order to master this, we must take a look at the problems and situations and develop an action plan to get us from where we are to where we want to be. By doing this, it creates the personal accountability for the vision and drive, motivation and will power to make it happen.

3. **Avoid becoming dislodged.** We must believe in the vision so strongly that we cannot be dislodged! Sometimes it may be that we have to back up the vision. That is, go back to the current reality for a brief moment and look at the situation and stop making excuses. For example, you want to have a successful business, you might back up the vision and realize that you have not made a phone call this week and networked with any potential clients. The reality is to back up momentarily, focus on the vision and realize that in order to build a successful business; you have to be more proactive and make those phone calls, follow up and follow through!

Habits and skills are very helpful to have, but when old habits and skills no longer fit new situations they can be our enemies. However, habits are crucial for change because it allows us to do things simultaneously. Many of the habits we have are good, but when we make a drastic change in our lives, such as kicking an addiction, getting a new job, getting married, getting out of prison; the old habits that worked for us in the old environment can be a major barrier in the new environment. They may not fit into our new experiences and in many instances debilitate our success.

For example: Deciding to lose weight and getting into shape. Once you have made the decision to lose weight and get in shape, the bad foods that you ate previously that caused you to gain weight is no longer a part of your diet. And, to maintain your new healthy lifestyle, you can't eat what others are eating all the time. This can be an uncomfortable feeling, especially being in the presence of people who are not as health conscious as you. My point is: you have to remove yourself from the environment where people are eating badly because you increase your temptation for eating badly as well.

The same principle applies to the acquired skills that we have developed from learning how to crawl, walk, riding a bike, and driving a car; all began as a conscious process of thought. It is a process. Through repetition and practice our skills become automatic. When we change our goals or our environment, old skills can cause us problems and limit our progress of success.

For example:

Expectations that we have in our lives has a powerful influence on what actually happens. This is because what we expect controls how we behave. The way we think about situations literally can affect our outcomes on life, both in a positive and negative way. Many people do an injustice to themselves because they defeat themselves before they try or nevertheless give themselves a chance. We beat ourselves up so badly that in many cases, we lack the confidence, faith and desire to pursue that dream, create that vision and stay the course to reaching our goals and success.

My point is: what you put into life is simply what you will get out. And the same applies to the expectation that others have of you. We try and live up to the expectations of others and find that many of those expectations are unrealistic, unimportant and truly have no room for future plans or goals. Not until we realize that the only important expectations are the ones that we have set for ourselves, then we realize that there are enough real barriers to change and growth without creating more because of negative expectations.

Don't' let the expectations of others cause you to begin to living up to them. Your actions will truly speak to your performance. At some point its' like becoming a fortune teller.....we usually get what we expect and that can be a major problem!

If we expect nothing less than the best, then that's exactly what we will get. It makes the difference between you reaching your goals in your personal and professional life. If you are always expecting to overcome the obstacles and challenges in life, then you will. Even during those major setbacks, you are still able to make a comeback. Have you wondered why some people are able to prevail over life's challenges more than others? It's because they do not allow expectations of others, self-pity and other irrational thoughts create negative reactions to their life's situation.

All the time, I come in contact with people who I viewed to be smart, creative and have more to contribute to society, but for some reason, they have allowed society, their past and current situations to become the barrier that limits their progress in life. Now that may be my expectation of what I think that they should be doing, however, the biggest question is; if I can see these disparities in them, why can't' they?

Likewise with situations where we all expect the less; we get it. You know the people, not you, but those that have truly defeated themselves every time they speak. "Well Bob, in the past I have never had my dream job, I guess I will never get it". "I know that I am skillful at what I do, but the big breaks never happen for me, they happen for everyone else" or you don't' understand that I come from a dysfunctional family and no has ever achieved anything in life"

These and other negative thoughts and statements are what some of us expect. And guess what? Others expect them of you too! That's right, I said it. A lot of people have low expectations of themselves so they may have them for you. You have heard the saying "if you expect to fail, you will" I am not sure who created that statement, but its' absolutely true. Stop expecting less than the best. Regardless of life's challenges and obstacles or the past experiences of life; get rid of those negative, debilitating thoughts and begin to embed the expectations of nothing more than the best for yourself. Don't' allow the low expectations be a barrier to changing the way that you use to think.

There are two sayings that life has taught us that I disagree with; that experience is the best teacher and if it ain't broke, then don't' fix it. However, I do believe an experience can be a good teacher because it allows us to think critically and make better choices and judgments and can keep us from making the same mistakes over and over again.

Likewise, nothing has to be broken with you for you to make changes in your life. I don't need to use drugs to know that it is addictive and deadly and ruins your mind, body and spirit. The same applies to making changes in your life, even if there is nothing currently wrong with it.

The challenges, obstacles and barriers of everyday life are just that; a part of life. The good thing is that you are not the only one that experiences them. Everyone has or will be faced with challenges, barriers and obstacles that will force them to make changes in their lives. The problem arises when you are in denial; especially when you are in denial about the fact that you need to make changes in your life, but refuse to. Denial about the need to make changes in your life is equally bad as an alcoholic or drug addictive who denies he has an addiction. It is the type of denial that can and will eventually stagnant your life.

Furthermore, the unwillingness to make changes in your life is just plain ridiculous! Because the world is continuously changing, you will be left behind. You might even know some people that are being left behind simply because they are not changing fast enough. And that is scary! Not only does the world require us to change, it does it at a very rapid pace. Technology reminds us all the time about the need to change. I can remember back when we had pagers as a means of communication. If you left your pager at home, you panicked and had to have it.

Today, the technology of the PDA's and cell phones have us almost in a state of panic where we believe that we cannot go anywhere without them. In fact, technology has contributed to people becoming lazier and lazier and unwilling to change. Nevertheless, that should not be an excuse for you.

Today is the day you have decided that you are going to take those challenges, barriers and obstacles and do something about them. You are going to finally commit to bringing yourself out of that comfort zone and realize that God gave each and every one of us the ability to go after our dreams and goals. I know, but......Blah, Blah, Blah and the hits just keep on rolling. Stop procrastinating and using the same old excuse as to why you have not begun to make the necessary changes in your life.

The challenge is yours

To challenge ourselves, we have to make a conscious decision about making a change in our life. That alone is a major challenge. And with these challenges comes some physical and emotional challenges as well. Many times we experience those changes, are aware of them, but ignore them. That too, is also a serious challenge. The challenge that I want you to do first is identify the actual change to be changed. You know the challenge that has been holding you back for so long that you are dying to do it, you just have not.

What I am asking you to do is to challenge yourself. The challenge is truly yours. If you never challenged yourself, you will never realize or reach your full potential in life. I know, you say to yourself, but I am doing okay. Well, you know as well as I do that okay means mediocre or marginal, and you are not a marginal person.

Not if you are reading this book. The people that are reading this book are those who first were attracted to the title of this book; secondly, realized after reading the introduction that this is the book for them. And these are the same people that have been the shouda, coulda, woulda that never amounted to reaching their full potential and success that they deserved.

I challenge you today to challenge yourself at changing something that you have always wanted to be or do in life. No matter how big or small, how long or short ago, but something that has not happened for you because you were unwilling to make a change. As I have always said in the past; the first step to making any change is the willingness. I want you to forget all about that. For some people, the challenge may be so overwhelming that you don't give yourself a chance.

However, I must caution you about a few things that will occur as a result of challenging yourself and making the change that you want. For example, let's say that you are attempting to kick an addiction. You will experience both a physical and emotional strain. Because an addiction is something that we HAVE to do daily, the decision to kick it sends a message to both the mind and the body. So you may experience some physical changes along with the emotional changes. And the reason for these side effects both physically and emotionally is because change is stressful.

First, it brings us out of that comfort zone. It separates us from people, places, situations, brings out the uniqueness in us. And most of all, it can create a mirror affect; that is; it has others beginning to take a close look at themselves and possibly decide to make changes as well. And that can be a good thing. Once you have made some changes, others see them, respect them and begin to follow what you have done. Oh, and that's another reason that I forgot to mention why people are afraid to change; it's not immediate, it takes time.

If one of your challenges have been to leave your job and get a better one, or start your own business, stop talking about it, put the fear aside and challenge yourself. You will never know if you can get a better job, start that business until you put yourself through the challenge. I know, people told you that you have to have money to make money, or that market is declining and people don't' need this and don't' need that etc… I have a saying "find a need a fill it". There is a need for everything in this world. The challenge will be if you believe and have the magnetic fortitude to face the challenges that are needed to fill those needs.

If one of your challenges has been that you become a better parent, husband, sibling, friend, coworker, boss or just a more productive person in life, the challenge is yours. Just focus on something that you have not been able to accomplish and begin to challenge yourself to make it happen!

Like many people who want to go into business for themselves, the fear of failure, anxieties about how to pay their bills or take care of their family is usually what keeps them from moving forward. And I am not saying that these are not legitimate concerns, because they are. However, if you are serious about making a change in some area of your life, you have to challenge yourself. Most people think because they failed at a business that they are likely to fail at it again. Not true, and those are the same people that never got back out there to really challenge themselves beyond that failure.

So what you failed. So what you thought you could make it and you realized that your plan of action or blueprint was not that million dollar plan that you anticipated, so what? Life is really about a challenge and how able and willing you are to defeat them. The more you challenge yourself, the closer you will get to reach your goal or dream. Time will pass and the world will get tired of beating up on you and the defeat of your challenges will come to past.

Get out of the comfort zone

Our comfort zone can keep us from changing and succeeding. It does exactly what it says; makes us comfortable and places us in a zone. And that zone prohibits us from developing and openness to change. We become so comfortable with our lives that we are in a zone as if we are aliens. I know, it's comfortable when you have a steady pay check coming in weekly or when you go home and that someone is there for you, or even when you take for granted the things that you have and not thank God for your Blessings.

It's not until life takes a turn for the worse and knocks us down so hard that we can't get up do we realize that we're in a zone. Or when we lose our job, can't pay the bills, or our relationship with that someone ends and we act as if life is over, or we now decide that because we are so down, now is the time to go to church and ask God to help us out. My point is, get out of the comfort zone. Prepare and act as if your job is on the line, if your relationship is rocky, either get counseling and work it out or leave, and if you are only comfortable with praying when things are going right in life, now is the time to challenge to change.

Whether we are doing better than we think we should be or worse, we get the same feedback. It's the difference that makes the difference! Only when you remove yourself out of that comfort zone will you begin to see differences in your life. As long as we stay complacent and comfortable about not making changes in our lives, we are limiting our chances to grow.

Put on your Armored Gear

"For our struggle is not against flesh and blood, but ...against the spiritual forces of evil... Therefore put on the full armor of God,"
Ephesians 6:12-13.

Facing the challenges and obstacles requires the appropriate protection; both emotionally and physically. You may be one of those persons that your kindness has been taken for weakness. You know, you have received the short end of the stick in spite of giving your all in all for a person or job. Your mind will begin to play games with you. You will begin to question yourself, your abilities and your self-worth. You may even ask yourself; is making this change really worth it? And you and only you can answer that question.

To ensure that you will be able to withstand the turbulence of the storms that will come your way, remember this; every time you make a conscious decision to change something about you or your situation in life, it will be difficult. You have to become tough, no non-sense and be ready to fight the battle. However, a challenge is not a challenge unless some form of change is in the making. Just as you are taking on the challenge, if there are no struggles, there is no progress!

Choose whatever it is to use as your armor, with the exception of a weapon. That armor may be as simple as the creation of a positive mindset, or the removal of certain people out of your life that have been a barrier in the past. And although the removing of people out of your life may be difficult and takes time; focus on the positive outcomes and benefits that you will reap if you do this.

My armor is God. He has been my protector through the toughest of the tough times. And still is my best armor today. Man will fail you every time; beware of those who appear to take an interest in you and appear to be supportive of you. This may not be the case for you. You may genuinely have a supportive family, friends, associates and colleagues. But the saying is"; those that are closest to us can be our worse enemy".

Here's a cautionary note: Your armor should be used as a protector only, not an excuse to close people out of your life or never to let down your guard. As we all know, we have to sometimes take off the armor in order to receive the Blessings of God and to be receptive to change. Those protective armors that you used in the past and did not work; change them. Create armored gear that will protect you and ensure the barriers to change are not holding you back.

The following exercise is what I call limited potential pitfalls. They are things that I limit when I am unable to break the barriers and challenges to change. They limit my growth and ability to change holistically. And in the end, if I am unable to change and break those barriers, others are affected. Place yourself and your limitations in the broken promises boxes and look at the areas in which your growth has been limited.

Limited Potential Pitfalls

Family Relationships	Hopes and Dreams	Health and Physical abilities

Job Skills	Personal /Spiritual Growth	Limited my........

The following is an exercise to begin to address your problem as you see it. It is imperative that you complete the exercise and be honest with yourself. Remember, it's not about someone else, it's about you and the barriers that you are facing that keeps you from making certain changes in your life. Use the exercise as a means to track where you are now and where you would like to be in the future. Give yourself four to six weeks between doing the exercise again.

Barrier:

Current Situation:

Habits:

Skills:

Beliefs:

Attitudes:

Expectations:

Act 4

Finding Your Life with Purpose

God granted us all with various gifts and talents. But God is omniscient (He is all-knowing). When you include God, or better yet, put Him first in the process of finding out your purpose, you are coming to someone who has the whole picture before Him. He already knows your future and has a specific plan for you. He knows all the pieces of the puzzle of your life and already sees how they should be connected.

I encourage you not to waste a moment more! Talk to God, pick up His manual, the Bible, and start to read it. My grandmother used to say it relentlessly but it was not until I was much older did I understand what she meant by; (Matthew 7:8 says,) "For everyone who asks receives; he who seeks finds; and to him who knocks, the door will be opened." What is your purpose in life? Many people spend their entire life and never truly discover what their purpose is in life. I think most of us realize after experiencing life's trials and tribulations that we really are not doing what our purpose is. And for many people, it becomes a daily struggle; it can affect their jobs, their relationships both family and friends.

Imagine for a moment that you're building a house. You hire a building contractor, but he never consults the blueprints drawn up by your architect, your designer. He works without a plan. An unwise move–because the contractor needs to know where to lay the foundation, erect the walls and place the windows. Only then will the home look the way it was intended.

The same can be said of life. How can we try to build our life without first consulting the great architect of life, the one who created us for a wonderful purpose? The Bible says, "We know that God causes everything to work together for the good of those who love God and are called according to his purpose for them" (Romans 8:28).

Furthermore, there is more to be gained by living according to God's plan. True fulfillment and meaning in life is found in God. That's why the philosopher St. Augustine said centuries ago, "You have made us for yourself, O God, and our hearts are restless until they find their rest in you."

By asking Jesus–God's son–to be the biggest part of your life, you will discover the very purpose for which God created you. There is nothing and no one else who can do this–no religion, no philosophy, no person. Just Jesus; He said of himself, "I am the way, the truth and the life. No one comes to the Father except through me" (John 14:6).

In my opinion, the purpose of life is to live to give. It is the key to a life unbound excitement and abundance. That is, giving back and helping others. That's what our calling really is. The world really is not about you and I, (although some of us think the world revolves around us, it does not!) Because Jesus died for us to live, it is an understatement that we should be constantly giving back.

Why is this concept difficult to grasp? Is it that people are so narcissistic that we forget why we are here on earth? Or is it that people are so comfortable with their lives and purpose is the last concern for them? Many people claim that they are not selfish and really do want to give back and help people, but the bottom line in many cases is each man for himself. And family is just as guilty of narcissistic behavior as well. In fact, family can be one of the biggest hypocrites when it comes to support and help.

I travel all over the world holding seminars and providing motivational speeches to people on various topics from inspiration, motivation, overcoming obstacles and making changes in lives to achieve happiness and success and one of the staggering questions that people pose to me all the time is; how did you find your purpose in life? They say, I can't seem to discover why I am on this planet, what my purpose is and that I don't seem passionate about anything. In my opinion, these are mere lame excuses and complaints to not attempting to seek out their purpose.

Because seeking our passion requires us to step outside of our comfort zone and state of complacency. We have become so fearful of what may happen if we really discover our purpose in life. What people will think, how to fulfill it and what steps to take to get started are all legitimate reasons. However, that alone is scary! To know that being in the comfort zone has so many people relying solely on what they think life's purpose is rather than their true passion of life. Discovering our passion and purpose is vital to our joy and well being. The problem arise when so many people have lost touch with any sense of their passion and purpose and have no idea how to access this information.

That is easy to say; but, for many people, it is easier said than done. It seems like the great majority of people tend to go through life without any real sense of purpose while vainly struggling for some imagined ideal of material success. And the question of success is clearly identified uniquely by each individual. However, if you know your purpose of your life and you are living it, then you may consider yourself purposeful.

If you honor the God given qualities of your life and all of his creation, you are living on purpose and with purpose. On the other hand, if you are not spiritually connected and are not thankful of the Blessing from God, purpose can be useless. You think that you have achieved a certain level of success in life because you have worked so hard that it finally happened? I agree with part of that equation; hard work, dedication leads to success, however, God gave you the ability to be motivated, stay focus, believe in yourself and persevere through the daunting tasks that you faced while getting to the top. And if you don't' believe that you should probably stop reading the rest of this book.

Your choice of what your purpose is should be as sacred as your personal relationship with a higher spiritual connection. Whether you are a Christian or not, purpose should evolve from a divine spirit.

I know so many people that are so talented and gifted; however, they never put those talents and gifts to use. Just imagine for a moment if we really used the talents and gifts that God gave us, how many people lives that we could save. Of course you may be a person that is not necessarily interested in saving lives, but if you are reading this book, there is probably a chance that you care something about the well-being of people.

You know those people at work or school that are really smart, but are wasting their intelligence on everything but what their true purpose is. They use lame excuses that are just alibis to their shortcoming. And you may be the total opposite and realize what your purpose is, but may be having some anxieties or difficulties in pursuing them. It's funny that other people can sometimes see a higher potential or purpose than we, and that may be because we are the most critical and cynical of the self.

For years as a young kid and even through my young adulthood I always had an interest in helping people. The care for and well being of others has always been something that I wanted to do. But it was not until I discovered that I could inspire and help change people lives that I really began to pursue my purpose in life. In other words, it has been my calling for a long time. It wasn't a coincidence or by chance (neither in which I believe in) that every job I held or educational interest had to do with helping others. God placed that interest in me at an early age. And he has done the same for you. But many people are blind to the talents and gifts that God has given us. Instead, we try everything else except what our purpose is.

One of the main problems is; people don't listen to and are not receptive to Gods messages. In fact, I think that we all have had messages sent to us from God, but for some odd reason, we fail to act or listen to them. Instead, we go on in life thinking that we are here by chance and not faith and that our success is based on the hard work and dedication that we gave to finding truly what our purpose is. And to some degree, I think that has some validity. However, at what cost and sacrifice are we willing to go far beyond what we are doing right now in our lives in pursuit of what our purpose really is?

Now you may have asked yourself now or in the past, what is my purpose? Guess what? You are asking the wrong person. We all have done this. We tell our family, friends, and co-workers and even our therapists how unhappy and disappointed we are with our lives, jobs and even our purpose in life. However, they can't help you. They can only advise you. And be careful with some people's advise; especially those that have not found their own purpose in life.

Think back to the jobs you held in the past. The impact you had on people or the company that you worked for. It was you that helped get that big contract or increased the sales of the company that brought them not only the money but the recognition as a credible company. And it's not a coincidence that every job you held in some capacity or another that you did your best, but still was not happy. Your talents and skills were still overlooked. Maybe it is because people really don't appreciate your work and you. Or maybe you should be doing the type of work that your purpose in life is calling for.

Don't ignore these messages and uneventful experiences in life. They are the messages from God telling you to use the talents that he gave you. Listen, take heave and act. Start to move into the direction that God wants you to be in. By now you probably have already discovered what you are good at. Well, if not, it's not too late. In fact, it's never too late. And if you are a younger person, that is, under the age of 20, you still have plenty of time. Even if you are an elder person, you have a purpose. Use it, don't waste it. You know the saying; it's better late than never is so true. You will not realize what an impact you could make on someone's life if you do what your purpose is.

Did you know that it is known that people change careers at least 3 to 5 times before realizing what their purpose is? I did. It was not a coincidence that I was in the Army, a police officer, a counselor, a professor and now an author and motivational speaker. It was always my passion; I just had not discovered it. However, if you noticed, all of the previous jobs that I held were in the line of helping people. Not only was it my interest, it was my passion, more importantly my purpose!

After speaking engagements people always come over to me and say, "I want to do what you are doing or I am trying to leave this job or get into this field, or I am so sick and tired of my job". And I think that they are looking for some magical answer, but I never give them one, I simply tell them to follow their passion and purpose. If you do that I can guarantee that you will not only get the job you deserve, but will love doing your job. And for many people, loving their jobs is out of the question. In fact 85% of the people hate their jobs. That means only 15% of people are living their dreams, serving their purpose and are passionate about their jobs.

You don't have to take my word on this, just begin with your family, friends and co-workers and ask them if they are serving their purpose in life. You will get answers like; I'm just doing this job until I find another one, or I need this job to pay the bills, or the money is too good, or it's hard to find another job. Most of the excuses you will get from them will not be because I am serving my purpose.

Now, there are people that are serving their purpose but still may be unhappy with the job. There are times when people have a passion and are serving their purpose and the environment may not be pleasant, the money may not be that good, or there is not much room for upward mobility. In cases like this, I suggest people be patient and find something else to continue serving their purpose. And I must stress this; money, status, prestige and titles are not elements of serving your purpose. Of course, it would be nice to make the money you want or be the CEO of that company that you want to work for, but it's not a necessity. Remember this; if you are serving your purpose, everything else will follow.

God not only wants you to serve your purpose, but He also wants you to prosper at it too. Never let anyone undermine your purpose of life. If you have a dream, a vision or goals and aspirations, don't let anyone talk against it or you out of it. And we all know that the people closest to us can do the most harm to us. Don't ask me why, but the bible states that.

Now I am not going to attempt to find your purpose for you. As a life coach and motivational speaker I am not the one to advise you either. You have to get that answer from God. My grandmother use to say "ask and ye shall receive". And I truly believe that if you ask God what is your purpose in life, he will let you know. It may not come as quickly or as specific as you would like (or maybe) but my point is; He will show you the way to your purpose. Just be patient and wait on him and you will definitely get the right answer.

Think back for a minute of at least the last 5 previous jobs that you held and ask yourself; was it really what I wanted to do? Or was it a title, money or a certain level of status or prestige that led you to the job, and, held on to that job for so long? I bet out of those 5 jobs, 3 of them made you sick and tired of being tired, right? So why didn't you do something about it? Were you afraid that you wouldn't find a comparable job? Or is it that you really wanted to go after your passion and purpose but was afraid to take the necessary steps to begin the journey?

If you have answered yes to at least 2 of the five questions, then now is the time to begin to find your purpose. Unfortunately, one of the many pitfalls to finding your purpose is trial and error. You know, you tried one thing and it turned out to be an error and felt as if you wasted time and energy on something that was by no means important to you. I always tell people that one way to finding your purpose is to ask yourself; is this going to benefit another person? Because the world is not about you and me, it is our duty and responsibility to help another. Now that is not my saying, it is written in the bible. Jesus sacrificed so much and died for us to do his work. Of course if you are narcissistic and don't care about anyone but yourself, then you would disagree with me.

One profession that I have discovered that people are very passionate about is teaching. After a few years of teaching both in secondary and higher education, I too realized that I had a passion for teaching. The dedication, hard work, patience and caring that is involved in teaching is truly a passionate as well as compassionate profession. And those teachers that are not passionate usually are the ones that don't stay around very long. Teachers have a kind heart and truly are the ones that impact children's lives. And while teaching was coinciding with my ability to speak to people through motivation, it all culminated to where I am today.

And that's what you have to do. It does not matter if you are a CEO of a fortune 500 company or a worker at McDonald's (not undermining working at McDonald's either) how you develop your passion is clearly what you have a desire for. And I hope that it is in line with the principals of a higher spirit. For example, the CEO may be making a million dollars or more a year, but may be unhappy at how he is making it. Yeah, it may seem nice to see the big bucks rolling in, but we all know that money does not make you complete. It's the things that you do for people, how you do it for them, and the reason it which you do it.

If McDonald's is your passion, be the best cook or person that is there. Just keep in mind that God wants you to prosper, so you should always strive for better. Go after a manager's position, and even one day owning a franchise. Wouldn't it feel great to have moved up from a cook to owning a store and still fulfilling your passion as well? So start thinking, feeling and finding what your passion is today!

Discovering your purpose can define your life

By knowing your purpose, it can define what you do and don't' do. You use it as a standard way of choosing what things you look at as vital and those that are not. You have to ask yourself, am I fulfilling my purpose for me and for God? Without a clear purpose or passion, you continue to make changes in your life over and over again. Here are a few tips on discovering your passion and defining your purpose in life.

1. <u>Is there something you already love doing</u>?-God distinctively embedded us all with innate characteristics and interests. The question: is it a hobby, or something that you passionately loved doing as a child, but never considered it as a possibility? For me, it has always been helping others. From early childhood to currently serving as a speaker and writer, my passion has always been helping those in need of service. Whether it's working with children, helping the elderly, volunteering as a mentor or actively involved in your church community; you probably could discover a way you could do it for a living.

   Open a community center for disadvantaged children, visit the elderly and assist the staff with weekly outings, or become a part of the ministerial staff at your church. If there's already something you love doing, you're ahead of the game. Now you just need to research the possibilities of making money from it.

2. <u>What do you spend hours reading or thinking about?</u>-For myself, when I get passionate about something, I'll read or talk about it for hours on end. I'll buy books and magazines. I'll spend days on the Internet finding out more. There may be a few possibilities here for you … and all of them are possible career paths. Don't close your mind to these topics. Look into them.

3. <u>Set some measurable goals</u>- Nothing can be attained without some set goals. **"With no plan….then plan to fail!"** Well, get out a sheet of paper, and start writing down ideas. Anything that comes to mind, write it down. Look around your house, on your

computer, on your bookshelf, for inspirations, and just write them down. There are no bad ideas at this stage. Write everything down, and evaluate them later.

4. <u>Do some research-</u> go to the library, search the internet and ask other people who are already working in your area of interest. Know as much about your passion as possible. If this has been a passion for a while, you may have already been doing this. At any rate, do even more research. Read every website possible on the topic, and buy the best books available. Find other people, either in your area or on the internet. The following are some questions to consider:

How much money do they earn? What training and education did they need? What skills are necessary? How did they get their start? What recommendations do they have? Often you'll find that people are more than willing to give advice.

5. <u>Don't fire your employer yet!</u> If you find your calling, your passion, don't just turn in your resignation tomorrow. It's best to stay in your job while you're researching the possibilities. If you can do your passion as a side job, and build up the income for a few months or a year, that's even better. It gives you a chance to build up some savings (and if you're going into business for yourself, you'll need that cash reserve), while practicing the skills you need.

6. <u>Never give up-</u> People who are passionate about anything never quit. Can't find your passion at first? Give up after a few days and you're sure to fail. Keep trying, for months on end if necessary and you'll find it eventually. Thought you found your passion but you got tired of it? No problem! Start over again and find a new passion. There may be more than one passion in your lifetime, so explore all the possibilities. Maybe you found your passion but haven't been successful making a living at it? Don't give up. Keep trying, and try again, until you succeed. Success doesn't come easy,

so giving up early is a sure way to fail. Keep trying, and you'll get there.

Program Your Mind For Success!

Act 5

"FAILURE LIES NOT IN THE FALLING DOWN BUT IN THE STAYING DOWN"

Success is 99% failure

Decide….Commit…..Succeed

Sometimes decisions have to be made that will ultimately determine the fate of our lives, our families, careers, our health and even our souls. I'm certain that at this point in your life you have experienced at least two of these five areas in life. And if you haven't, get ready cause its coming. Hopefully you have at least made the decision to ask God for forgiveness for your sins and have accepted Jesus Christ as your Lord and savior. In other words, you are saved. Some are more afraid than others about making decisions, other make decisions and think nothing of it. I guarantee you that those people who are able to make decisions readily are more likely to achieve their goals, reach their success and have more productive and stable lives. Here are some steps you can consider when making decisions:

Deciding to become successful- is the first step towards reaching the success you want. The willingness has to be here. As my grandmother always said" where there's a will, there's a way. Do your best and forget about the rest. A decision has to be firm, consistent and of good judgment regardless the outcome. You are more likely to succeed at whatever you want if you truly make a decision to do so.

Ask God is it in His plan- before you make that decision. In the past I have been guilty of not including God in my decision making process and paid a serious price for it. He wants you to come to Him for advice and questions. *"Ask and Ye Shall Receive"*. Remember He already knows the outcome of that decision before you even make it. So why not at least give Him the benefit and respect and include Him.

List the advantages and disadvantages- of the decision and what are the ramifications if I do and do not make this decision. You may have questions such as; what if I fail, what will people think? How long will it take? And do I truly have what it takes to make it happen. Only you can answer these questions. Remember, sometimes we can be our worse enemies but also our best antidotes.

Do some research- the internet is the most powerful search engine in the world. Go search and see what others have done to make decisions in accomplishing their goals. If possible, talk to others and ask about sacrifices they had to make when making a decision about something. Try and talk to appropriate people, not people who have talked the talk, but people who have walked the walk and proven results. If possible, seek advice from friends and family, but again be careful about who you get your advice from. Everyone may not have your best interest.

Be receptive to new ideas and begin to think outside the box- Listen, be patient and be open. At times, God gives us stepping stones before we get to the top. Don't totally eliminate other opportunities to make decisions even when it may not be aligned directly with what you are trying to do. For example, if God gave you the gift to be a great teacher and you have been contemplating ministry, but because others say you can't be a preacher, you close your mind to other teachings.

Recognize that there are no right reasons for making a particular decision- The fact that a particular path is important to you, regardless of what others think, legitimizes it. The only way you will know if you made the right decision is to make a decision first. If you don't make a decision, you still have made a decision; so make a decision. Think honestly about any fears, motives or biases guiding your thinking but don't get bogged down to a point where it takes you out of focus and interferes with your ability to make a decision.

<u>Don't allow your feelings to overrule your decisions.</u> This is when many people get soft and weak. They allow their feelings to be a distraction, ultimately affecting their ability to make that decision. Don't get me wrong, you don't have to be cruel to people, but you have to learn to be firm and toughen your skin, it's a tough world and people will take your kindness for weakness.

<u>Plan-Those who fail to plan, plan to fail</u>- No if and buts about it. With careful planning, you can sort of plan for any possible repercussions that may follow your decisions. You have no way to definitely predict the outcomes of most decisions but a good plan goes a long way.

<u>Make the decision</u>- I mean really make a decision. For example, you have been avoiding your boyfriend/girlfriend for days because you don't want to be with him anymore. Rather than making a decision to communicate with him to tell him it's' not working out, you lead him on to thinking that things are okay. You stay miserable, isolated and non-communicative and it gets worse. Make the decision to communicate and let him know that you are unhappy and its' not working out. It's a decision that you can live with and you are happier in the long haul.

One final take: How are you going to succeed at something and you can't make a simple decision. That may sound harsh, but if I am talking to or about you; get over it. You have to stop making excuses why you can't do something. Stop blaming others for your shortcomings and stop putting off the decision to make that decision. That is the decision to finally go after your dreams, reach your goals and finally use your God-given talents. So what if you fail: so what that you don't know the outcome, so what if John, Bob and Mike failed. Just as our trials and tribulations are different from each other, likewise are our distinct talent and abilities are different. Success does not happen overnight nor does the ability to make sound and concrete decisions occur overnight.

Making a decision is like saying; I am, I will and I can be successful. It's like anything else, it begins with a simple thought, and then the actions are likely to follow. This fundamental premise may be an explanation to why so many people who lack the ability to make a decision also lack the confidence, belief and willingness to achieve success.

I hear people say all the time that they have not made a decision to something. I respond to that saying with the same ole' saying" not deciding to do something is an actual decision not to do something. In other words, when you don't make a decision to do something…you actually do nothing. You know people who can't make a decision about anything. I'm not talking about asking for opinions or advice, but coming to a conclusion and taking a chance on making a decision even if we don't know the outcome.

With that in mind, decide what it is that you want to change. How in the world are you going to change something until you have made the decision to change? It is not possible to make any changes to anything in life unless we first make a conscious (thought provoking) decision to change whatever it is that we want to change. The problem with many people is they don't seem to know how to make a decision.

Here's my advice; think of something that you really have wanted to do but for whatever reason you never began or started and never completed. And ask yourself the question; why? Why haven't I begun to do what I really want to do? And before you answer the question, list all of the excuses you used that kept you from making that decision. The reality is; there is no excuse for not making a decision. God equipped us all with certain qualities and talents and we all have a brain, so use it!

Some critics claim that people who can make decisions are considered to be leaders. To some degree, I disagree. However, it's a choice and the willingness that you are to make the decision. It does not take a general to make a decision on something that you know you want to do or accomplish. Everyone should have goals and hopefully some vision and direction about what they want to do in life. If you don't know, go back and read chapter 2 in this book on purpose in life.

Most people fail at something more than they succeed. In fact, successful people have failed so much that all they know how to do is succeed. They have endured the fear, pain and challenges that come with failure. After many attempts of going after a dream or goal and continuously failing and becoming discouraged, many people end up giving up. Only those patient and receptive to God's plan are those that will succeed. Strong willpower is not enough to succeed. You have to program that brain that God gave us all to do exactly what you want it to do. Every time you get down get back up; staying down means that you have given up. Just think where we would be if God gave up on us or if every time we committed a sin God said" no more forgiveness for you"; you have run out of chances with me".

In my opinion, success is falling in love with your passion. It is a passion about something that you are good at doing. I mentioned that because if you have a passion for what you are doing, you will *never work a day in your life!* Work wont' be considered work, it will be what you are enjoy doing. Unfortunately, many people are not working in professions in which they have a passion for. I am truly blessed; I am working in my area that I have a passion for, and I truly love it. Ironically, some people fail because they are afraid to succeed. Success brings on more responsibility, accountability and criticisms. The more successful you are, the more you are on the watchful eyes of others. Expectations from others on your success will be misconstrued by others, especially the ridicule and envious treatment from those haters. Sorry, but that's the way it is! As I mentioned earlier, if they criticized Jesus; imagine what they will do and say about you.

Unfortunately society creates an awful depiction of what life is; the notion that you are only successful if you have wealth and fame. Manifested through media, pop culture and common perceptions of people, directly or indirectly, society equates success only with the economics of life as if this is the only ground where a person evolves.

Liberal thinking says that life can simply be spelled as satisfaction. If you feel healthy, contented, happy, and fulfilled but not exactly wealthy, nobody can just say that you are not successful in life. You felt and dealt with your life exactly the way you wanted it because you are in total control and this satisfies your existence.

If you can only think as positively as this, you are assured of a clearer way in the future. But like many other endeavors, there are no straight roads only rocky roads with holes. There is no promise of immediate grandeur. You have to work your way towards satisfaction. It is not a sweet fruit on the tree ready to be picked. But, there is no cause for worry because maps and guides are provided for you to cling on as you take your journey to ultimate satisfaction in life.

Programming your mindset to a successful life is evident in your philosophies, principles and attitudes. What you believe in, stand for and willing to die for all can contribute to you failing or succeeding. And that's serious! Willing to die for! That's true foresight and sincerity. There is no better way to say it. It has to be embedded in your mind all the time. Create the positive mindset that will get you what you want. Remember, God created man to use the mind. All these encompass aspects of your life opens your chances to a satisfying life. Create a blueprint on how to get there. Positive philosophy, principles (what you practice, value), and attitude (optimistic or pessimistic) are essential to creating the mind for success. The following are a few tips to programming your mind for success:

Incorporate a healthy lifestyle- without health, you have nothing. The mind is a terrible thing to waste so use it sparingly. The body is your temple; treat it with care, take care of it and it will take care of you. I suggest limiting the amount of meat consumption and replace with more beans, veggies, nuts and fruits. It does not have to be a vegan diet, but a moderate change in your daily food intake affects your body as well as the spirit; we must believe in something or we'll fall for anything. When closely examining if your health is intact, ask yourself the following questions; how in touched are you with physically taking care of your body? Do you exercise regularly? How about your eating habits? A balanced fueled mind, body and spirit can help elicit a strong positive mindset. Likewise, a bad diet can cause both a psychological and physiological affect on you.

Activities: social and leisure time- Who do you spend your leisure time with? Is it with positive or negative people? Is it with people who share similar goals and plans as you? Or are you associating with people who are afraid of change, afraid to succeed, or don't want to see you reach your goals or success? Find a common ground that can be fun and productive at the same time. Make sure that you include in your leisure and social time those persons who share similar interests. Sometimes our leisure time can create faulty thoughts that can cripple our ability to creating a positive mindset.

Communication: It's okay to communicate with yourself. It's all a part of the creation of positive affirmations and self-talks. Ask yourself these questions; are you effectively communicating with yourself and others to help you affirm your thoughts of success? Or are you not able to communicate effectively because both your verbal and non-verbal communication skills are weak and often cause negative thoughts in your mind?

Knowledge: I know. You're smart, unfortunately you don't know everything. So ask yourself; are you receptive and willing to accept new information, especially knowledge from others who have become successful? Be willing and able to receive all the additional knowledge about something that you are attempting to do. People say that knowledge is power; I say "*Knowledge is potential power"* because once you have acquired knowledge, there is no limit to your potential. Be careful with who and what you receive your knowledge from.

Attitude: Attitude is everything. It is the driving force behind our thoughts, actions and beliefs. If your attitude sucks, you automatically create a catalyst to negative thoughts. Attitude and belief go hand in hand. If you have a bad attitude, it's likely going to bring negative thoughts towards success, but definitely will keep you in the rut of failure. As I previously mentioned, if you think you will fail, you will. Likewise, if you know you will win and achieve your success, you will!

Egypt in the Old Testament symbolizes a place of hardship for the Jews. It was a place where many of God's favorite people spent their time. Spending time in the desert however can be enlightening. Spending time there can rub you in the most uncomfortable way in order to awaken your inner self, allowing you to create a new person on the outside. One thing is certain; whenever you spend time in the desert consider that the situation will not last; that change is on the way. Change can send you swimming upstream to happiness or spiraling downhill with your back against a wall. Change can twist you up in a knot so painful, you wonder if God is angry with you and then He raises you up to motivate the world.

John C. Maxwell said, "It's possible to lose sight of your dream when you're working hard in the trenches. That's why it's important to always keep your eye on the big picture." Each day that God blesses you with breath, challenge and compete with yourself to see how much more you can fall in love with the art in your heart. It's not always easy you see. That passion for your work tends to take control and you may rub people the wrong way. How many emails have you received advising you how you should run your business their way? 'You need this in order to do that. Try this try that.' However, when that information rush occurs, back up and listen to your inner voice. Pray and ask God for guidance knowing that the art in your heart is dancing to a different melody.

Don't get me wrong we all could use assistance from others from time to time. However, building your foundation is a serious process. You have to choose excellent materials to ensure your building will stand strong over time. Be aware of quick fixes or fast company. Change is not always comfortable in either direction. Therefore, welcome a little power surge, positive or negative, to activate the art in your creative heart. I have learned also that rubbing one the wrong way will awaken you from your dead sleep when you're ready to open your heart's eyes. As a witness, sometimes that rub may force you to do so, ready or not.

Failure is not an option, it's a choice!

If you think you are going to fail….you will fail. How many times have you heard that saying? Probably many, and the average person still does not get it. It's not rocket science, just a basic premise, however, if practiced effectively, it can change the course of your life forever, either successfully or the experience of constant failure. At least the way you view it now. Well, maybe you are one of the elite group of people that have already created your own positive thinking and don't need any help with programming your mind for success, but I guarantee you if you read this book, you will be able to increase your positive thinking, ultimately bringing more success than you have now.

Self-mastery, the ability to have complete control over yourself and therefore, your destiny is the key to achieving any measure of success in life. One step toward self-mastery is belief in you. Our minds are often polluted by negative thoughts introduced by ourselves and others. To be successful, we must believe in ourselves and fill our minds with positive thoughts of success and achievement. One way to do this is with positive affirmations.

In the bible it says, "If you believe, all things are possible." Napoleon Hill said, "Whatever the mind of man can conceive and believe it can achieve." And Oscar Wilde said, "Yes; I am a dreamer. A dreamer is one who can find his way by moonlight and see the dawn before the rest of the world."

Our subconscious mind is an incredibly powerful tool that we can use to fashion success or failure. It will do what we tell it to do. It all depends on what thoughts we feed it. I strongly urge you to feed your mind with only positive thoughts. The following are some examples of positive affirmations you can feed your inner mind for success:

I will win because I do what is necessary to achieve my dreams.
I love and accept myself.
I love and care for my body and it cares for me.
I am constantly adding to my income.
I am worthy of love

Get out of your head and get into your greatness! I can think of no better way to do this than with positive affirmations. Repeat them to yourself often.

Reframing our language also allows us to fill our heads with the positive rather than the negative. Research suggests that 83% of the conversations we have with ourselves are negative. The benefits are enormous when we reframe our inner-communication to capture the positive perspective.

Here are a few examples of how you can turn your negative words (and the accompanying self-defeating thoughts) into positive communication (and self-empowering actions):

Instead of saying, "That's just the way I am," say, "I have decided to try a different approach."

Instead of saying "problem," call it an "opportunity." This allows for an improvement of the situation.

Always reframe your language so that you have control over what you do and who you are.

I know that you are brilliant, charismatic and motivated, but let's face it; everyone needs some help at times. You need help especially when the thinking of the average American is so faulty and irrational when it comes to positive thinking. Most people defeat themselves before they give themselves a chance.

In most cases, people actually do the reversal; they program their minds for failure. They think of all the past dispositions, past experiences(including those of others), obstacles that will come their way and make excuses about why it is impossible to reach their level of success and change the way they think. As a result, time passes them by and one day realized that shoulda, coulda, woulda never amounted to anything.

I know. Not you. The other person, the other excuse, obstacle, friend, and whatever reason is clearly not your alibi to where you are today in your life. In spite of what many people say, success is something that everyone wants. And believe it or not, both success and failure is only a second away. Remember this; ninety-nine percent of success is Failure! It takes so many times to fail, but only one time to succeed. And regardless of what obstacles and failures that come your way, you are truly a step away from achieving your success.

And trust me; I am not saying that it will take you ninety-nine times at trying whatever it may be that you are trying to do, but the concept is universal; ninety-nine times of failing, it only takes one time to succeed. And the only way that you won't gain your success is if you make the decision to stop pursuing it. Then you have automatically failed. And if you really want it, failure will not be an option.

The problem with some people (not you), is the quick fix that leads to long term failures. Just as it takes time to build any successful business, likewise, it takes time to program your mind for success. Why do you think that a computer appears to be so brilliant? It's not that the computer is such a genius, but the CPU has been programmed to do whatever the input requests. That is, the programmer programs the computer, ultimately to provide some outcome or information.

But what's wrong with the mind? You have heard the saying that *"a mind is a terrible thing to waste."* I would go even farther and say a *dream is a horrible thing to waste!* Why is it that we have such a difficult time in programming our minds to do whatever we want it to do? Is it because most of us fear the unknown? Are we afraid that if we become too programmed that we will develop a sense of complacency in our lives?

If there is something that you truly want in life but you are not sure how to go about it what do you do? Most people *dream* but don't *pursue* what it is that they want. If there is something that you really want in life, why don't you give it all you got and go after it?

Success is not obtained by people who *think* they can get it, it is obtained by people who *know* they can get it. People that are successful are successful because they refused to get caught up in the irrational thinking of the non-believers and achievers of success. In fact, they are the people that truly follow the passion and dreams that others are afraid of.

They have mastered their minds to obtain nothing less than success, failure is not an option! And if they do fail at something, they use the failure as a tool to gain the success they really want and deserve. And that's what you have to do when programming your mind for success. You have to understand the cause and effect of programming your mind. Remember this; once you have programmed your mind, the only thing left is the hard work. That is, your faith (believing that you can achieve it), the evaluation of the self, the sacrifices to be made, the determination, will power and perseverance all culminated into the process of programming the mind.

Creating the mindset of self-motivation

How we motivate ourselves? What motivates us and how do we keep ourselves motivated all depends on our mindset. That is, being able to create it constructively or restrictively. Once we experience a setback or challenge, how does it affect our mindset and attitude? As you may be aware, this is where most people change their attitude about how hard it is to create the motivation and keep it through the daunting times of setbacks and obstacles.

When I think about how I have been able to become motivated and stay motivated there are two concepts that come to mind; constructive and restrictive motivation. The constructive motivation allows me to take control of my own life. And the restrictive motivation takes away my drive and energy needed to self-motivate. I always tell people, "If it's to be….it's up to me! That means it is absolutely critical that I vividly visualize what I want in order to get excited and motivated enough to go after it. I am looking at where I am today, where I want to be tomorrow, which enhances my ability to choose how I will get there.

When I use constructive motivation I can see the actual pay value, not necessarily always the monetary compensation, but the emotional gratification as well. For example, when I began teaching life skills and job readiness to people transitioning out of prison or who have experienced major setbacks in life i.e., homeless, drug abuse, the pay value came from the impact that I had on changing the lives of the people in the program. I was at a government agency so the pay was not that great, but the impact of what I was doing for the people in transition was far more rewarding for me than the actual paycheck.

Using constructive motivation also allows you to see the picture to win. You see more possibilities, become more creative, have more energy and program your mind for nothing but positive outcomes. The big picture for me in teaching those life skills and job readiness was to transform and change the lives of people who needed motivation and inspiration. And you get a chance to visualize and create more opportunities for yourself that you had not thought of before. Out of teaching those life and job skills classes, I formed my own company providing the same service. I saw that it was an opportunity to change the way it was being done and do it slightly different. And in order to do that, I had created my own program.

On the other hand, restrictive motivation is generally based on some type of fear. We restrict our options and limit our mindset. And we do that by using the blaming game. Not taking accountability for our failures and shortcomings in life. You know the people that blame everyone for their loss and never, ever, hold themselves accountable for anything. It's always someone else fault, or situation that caused them to be in the position that they are in now. Restrictive motivation allows us to see the loss, but it does not motivate us to motivate ourselves. It does exactly what is says; restrict our thinking, lock out all possible solutions to being able to solve problems and limit our chances to comeback after a setback.

I must admit. I too was a victim of restrictive motivation in the past. I always found an excuse to find an excuse to find an excuse. And I realized that after trying to find the excuse to find an excuse, I never found it. My point is; until I realized that I was doing nothing but making excuses about something that I could have control over. And that control was my thinking. That is being able to create the positive mindset of constructive over restrictive motivation. Today, I will settle for nothing less than positive outcomes, regardless of what happened to me in the past (I will discuss later), I will never let it keep me down to a point where I can't stay motivated to reach whatever goals and dreams that I set.

The key to all motivation is to see the personal reward of what we are doing. It is very imperative to recognize how we talk to ourselves, both constructively and restrictively. Ingrain the "I want to rather than I have to"; to motivate you to reach your goals and dreams. You need to develop the habit of making your own choices....taking a look at all the options and then making the best choice to that problem or situation. Sometimes our choices are not always the best, but that is a part of maturing in life. However, there are choices, and if we don't make them, someone can and will make them for us.

When we restrictively motivate ourselves, we are basically saying that we don't have any control over our lives. "Its' not my fault" means that we are allowing others control our lives. You are basically saying" Okay, you win, I don't' know what else to do, so you choose for me". That's awful. How can you allow someone to make choices for you, especially when you have the ability to make them for yourself?

"If the only tool you have is a hammer,
You tend to see every problem as a nail"

Abraham Maslow

Some of the greatest barriers between the self and what we want our lives to be are like "bricks" of past negative experiences, negative self-talk that have restricted us and caused us to lack motivation, and prohibits us from accepting negative feedback from others as the truth. Take the short test to evaluate where you are in creating the positive mindset. Remember, it's your chose about how you go about motivating yourself. Are you a constructive or a restrictive motivator? Be aware of some of the barriers that restrict us from becoming self-motivated:

    A. Becoming depressed- "down in the dumps, got the blues, life's a bummer"

    B. Not being accountable- "it's not my fault", it was him/her, or them"

    C. Being a winner-" poor me, I never get the breaks"

    D. Unprepared-" no one ever hires an ex-offender, past drug abuser"

    E. Alcohol/drug abuse-" It's the only way that I can cope"

    F. Fighting with spouse-" I just can't' get along with her/him"

    G. Anger/hostility-" I can't resolve conflict"

    H. Neglect mental/physical health-" what's the use"

    I. Lazy-"what's the point, why should I try?"

    J. Lost opportunities due to poor attitude-"I'm not good enough, so why try?"

    K. Lost friends/relationships due to abuse/neglect-"I am better off without him/her"

1. What are some of the positive examples of how you have accomplished something because you where able to used constructive motivation?

2. Do you surround yourself around people who are restrictively or constructively motivated?

3. Do I use the self-talk method to create a picture of what I want or don't' want?

4. What factors can I incorporate in creating a positive mindset about what I want today and the decisions that I have to make to get to the future?

Creating the self-Talk motivation

"ARGUE FOR YOUR LIMITATIONS
AND SURE ENOUGH, THEY WILL BE YOURS"
-Richard Bach

I hear people say all the time; I can do it, but.....and the excuses go on and on and on to what they said they could do, never happened. So many times we limit our ability and short ourselves of the better things in life just by creating a negative self talk dialog. The power of the self-talk conversation can be one of the most powerful tools used in programming your mind for success. The self-talk is a conversation that we carry on in our minds where we judge and interpret our experiences. The self-image that we create and the picture we have of who we are that keeps us acting the way we see ourselves. It can make or break your ability to motivate yourself, nevertheless hinder your progress in obtaining your success. And finally, the self-talk serving as a simulator in our mind can create where we can practice new behaviors so we can control our own self-image, ultimately our own actions.

We store and record what we think about what we see; the truth as we see it. So if we decide to change or grow, this stored self-image that is formed can be a major obstacle and challenge to positive mind setting. Then when life's mishaps and setbacks occur, we begin to beat ourselves up and instead of exploring ways to overcome an obstacle or lift ourselves up; we embed a negative self-talk or pessimistic cycle in our minds.

For example, you say that you never get the good jobs. Other people are so lucky that they get the better paying job and you get the jobs with less pay and harder work. And in the past, this has been true. You are on your way to the interview and you are beginning to say these self-defeating things to yourself. Now you are at the interview and in the interview you are still thinking of defeat and using the past to say that you will never get a job like this. And guess what? You leave the interview, defeated, still pessimistic and doubtful about if you did a good job or will you even get the job. That same old self-defeating attitude carried on before, during and after the interview.

This type of thinking has to stop. You cannot go on with a self-defeating attitude about life. Your mind has to be programmed for nothing less that the best! God gave us all the opportunity to use our skills and abilities to be whatever it is that we want to be. But we have to be prepared in order to do that. Some of us are so convinced that we cannot reach that level of success that you envisioned that you never give it a shot.

Think back for a moment when you literally talked yourself out of a situation (bad or good) depending on what it was. What was the determining factor that caused the outcome? In that situation, your self-talk involved some form of self-talk to either get your point across or to motivate yourself or become unmotivated at something that you were trying to accomplish.

My point is; the self-talk motivation is controlled by you. Your tongue can be your worst enemy or your best antidote. Most of the time, your tongue literally got you in trouble. Instead of using the tongue to motivate yourself, you used it as an excuse that lacked the motivation or created a self-defeating state of mind. And when you thought back to that situation, you could remember what role your tongue played in creating that self-talk defeat.

Some people are good with talking a good game. You may say that some people can talk themselves out of any situation. That may be true, but there is no secret potion or methodology to it. It is not that the person has so much game in talking out situations, instead, they have mastered the ability to use the tongue in a way that it is convincing, and it sounds good. But the reality of it is that those people are generally the ones that are self-motivated, have a positive mindset and in most cases usually get what they want. These are usually the people in retail and sales jobs and part of their performance is to sell, sell, and sell. The more a salesman believes in his product, the better chance that he can convince the buyer to buy his product or use his service.

And maybe we should begin to take the approach of a good salesman. That is to talk and sell you into the positive mindset of a self-talker. With my first book, I became an unstoppable salesman. I use to go out and set up tables and talk to potential customers about my book and convince them to purchase a copy of it. I was a true salesman. I believed in my book, myself and have a passion for talking to people about changing their lives and becoming motivated. Never before had I imagine myself as a salesman. And sometimes, we posses qualities and have skills that we discover later on in life. This was definitely discovered later on in my life. I remember when I first began selling the first copies. I talked to so many people that I literally talked myself into believing that I could sell a copy of my book to George Bush!

I was conditioned into an optimistic attitude and a mindset that was settling for nothing but getting the results that I wanted; to sell my book. And I challenged myself even further. I said to myself; my quota each day is to sell 20 books. And if I don't' sell 20 books, I could not go home. I held myself to that and made it happen, if it meant staying outside beyond an eight hour time period, that's what I did. I made it happen. But it was because I was able to talk myself into accepting nothing less than that quota for the day. And that is what you have to do. Visualize your goals and dreams and talk to yourself on what measures you have to take and how you will motivate your-self for nothing but the best.

And it does not happen overnight. It takes time to acquire this type of skill. And I know what you are thinking; I am quiet and my personality is passive and I don't talk that much. None of those things have anything to do with you being able to use the power of the tongue to create the mindset that you need to make it.

On the other hand, the same self-talk applies to people who are unable to use the tongue as an antidote. It becomes a pessimistic rather than an optimistic approach to programming the mindset. It's like the creation of a simulator in our mind where we can begin to develop our greater potential. And sometimes, who and what we listen to affects our self-talk dialog. For example, one of the most powerful forms disseminating information is through the media. The impact of information through radio, television and the internet plays a vital role in creating the mindset in both the pessimistic and optimistic views on life.

And in spite of the social impact of the media, we have to hold or selves accountable for some of the pitfalls and mistakes in life. It is imperative that if we want to take control of how we think that we don't let ourselves or others dump garbage on us. We need to constantly protect ourselves from the negative thoughts and negative talk that have been built up in our minds. The goal is to take control of our self-talk and build self-image in order to control how we act.

Ask yourself; are you talking to yourself and others? How are the people in your circle talking around you to each other and about others? What positive comments are they contributing to painting their personal picture? If you are comfortable about the answers to these questions and they are reinforcing and helping to create a positive mind set for you, then you are more than likely to be in the right place and around the right people.

Give yourself a quick test. For the next 24 hours, make a decision to not put yourself or let anyone else put you down. Eliminate participating in any negative put downs, finger pointing, judgment of others or ridiculing. During the 24 hour no put down, ask and answer the following questions. Complete the self-concept exercise so that you can take a closer look at the accountability of the self. Be honest and don't skip any questions, remember in order to change your truth, it is absolutely necessary to control your negative self-talk and negative self-talk to others.

1. Who am I?

2. What can and can't I do?

3. What do I believe I can and cannot do?

4. What do I like the least and most about myself?

5. What kind of challenges do I choose to seek out?

List 3 ways to build personal accountability right where you are today

1.

2.

3.

List 3 affirmations that you could use to represent positive thoughts and add confidence to changing your mind set.

1.

2.

3.

List 3 ways to say something positive to self and others around you

1.

2.

3.

Once you have complete these two exercises, complete the contract below as an assurance that you are holding yourself accountable for either creating the positive self-talk and new mind set or still playing the blaming game. This contract can also be used as a reminder, a motivator and a reference to how far you have come in making the changes necessary in moving closer to your goals and reaching the success that you deserve!

My Contract with My self

I, _____ commit to changing my self-talk from negative to positive in the following 3 ways; (for example, instead of letting the past dictate my future, I will used it to motivate myself to moving forward rather than backwards.

1.

2.

3.

Signed:_____
Witness:_____

Date:_____

Act 6

"Use the Setbacks as a Setup to Comeback"

– Willie Jolley

One of the biggest setbacks in my life came when I formed an outpatient mental health clinic. It was not the actual fall of the clinic that was the major setback, but the repercussions that followed it. I had the opportunity to take my God-given talent and ability and impact the lives of people in need. Working as a psychologist and helping people to identify and address problems in their lives is priceless to me. The joy and gratification of seeing people transform is so rewarding that I can't find the perfect words to describe it.

I have been so blessed over the years to be able to recover from the setbacks, challenges, obstacles and failures and turn them into some positive outcomes. And I am not taking all the credit for it. God gave me the motivation and will power to excel and achieve even through the daunting tasks that were ahead after setbacks. And I have learned that in the process of recovering from a setback, it requires patience and involves a process. In other words, you just don't begin to recover from the setback without some concrete blueprint in place. You know the saying,"*If you don't plan, then you plan to fail!"*

The unfortunate thing about setbacks is they are, in most cases, unexpected and unknown. And they can be so detrimental that you can program yourself to stay down after you have been knocked down. Most setbacks take a major toll on the body, mind and spirit. It physically wears you down, can make you depressed, and can dampened your spirit and have you questioning God as to why this happened to you. You begin to question your abilities and if you will ever be able to make a comeback after this setback. And the people around you don't help either. They feel sorry for you, causing you to begin to feel sorry for yourself. And that is the worst thing that you can do. The more you feel sorry for yourself, the less likely that you will recover.

One of the most devastating setbacks that I have experienced so far happened when the outpatient mental health clinic that I had worked so hard to form had to close. It was not the mere fact of just closing, but the reason that it closed – accused of Medicaid fraud. I had become a victim of circumstance. I had partnered with another company who was providing similar services like my clinic. The only difference in the two companies was that my business treated patients with mental health disorders and the other business provided rehabilitative services, such as mentoring and tutoring. It was an opportunity of a lifetime; at least at the time that's what I thought.

Like most businesses, building a clientele and reputation usually is a difficult process. It takes time, dedication, sacrifice and taking many risks. I had completed my doctorate work in education and decided that I wanted to work for myself. I was teaching psychology at a couple of local colleges and felt that I could make more of an impact if I opened my own business. I think once you have the faith in God and yourself, you are able to do anything, even if you don't know the outcome. And with most people, the fear factor is what keeps them from going after that dream or starting that business.

I was introduced to a group of businessmen (as they called themselves) for the opportunity of growing my business. I had been in business nine months and had barely enough clients to even pay the rent to the office that I was renting. The two owners of the other company offered me an incentive to move my business and connect my services with them and that they would put up all of the initial money to finance the costs of moving the business to their location. With an opportunity to build up a strong client base and make more money, I thought that it was a great chance to take my business to the next level.

Unfortunately, I did not do my homework. I did not check out the people that I had gone into business with. I never checked to see if they were not in good standing with the department of taxation and assessment, nor did I check to see if they had been audited from the department of mental health and hygiene. Their company had already been in business for 15 months prior to our partnership.

They had a great reputation of providing rehabilitative services to children and adolescents. At least through my observation, everything appeared to be OK. Clients were being seen at all three of their locations, parents indicated that they were pleased with the services that were rendered, and the community seemed to be becoming a better place for those in need of mental health services.

They had the operation appearing to be working so smoothly that they even provided transportation to pick up clients and drop them off to ensure that the clients would be seen for services. They employed more than 200 employees who had appeared to be eager to make a difference in changing the lives of people. And that's truly what I had set out to do – continue to help those in need of mental health and life's transformations. I had gone to school and obtained all the education and training needed to do just that.

In February of 2003, I made a conscious decision to become self-employed. At the time, I was a professor at a local college and was working part-time at various local social service agencies. I decided that because I had a passion for helping people, I would open up an outpatient clinic to specifically help people with clinical disorders.

I began by opening up an office in Maryland. I had no money and no clients. In fact, I could not even afford the rent and phone bill. However, I convinced the landlord to allow me to stay there at the office. I marketed my business by soliciting as a mentor program while working on getting credentialed as an outpatient mental health clinic.

On my days off, I would go out and pass out brochures to various communities, other agencies and schools. After several months of working with five or less kids on mentoring and life skills, I was finally credentialed by the state to operate as an outpatient mental health clinic. It was in October of 2003 when I received my provider number. However, I still could not begin billing for Medicaid.

Still, with minimum clients and no funding to continue to operate, I had the provider number, but no staff licensed to provide the services. I began to recruit licensed and non-licensed social workers and counselors.

In November 2003, I was out marketing my program and met a young man who I had gone to college with. He was working for a company called the Better Project. The Better Project was a PRP Program (Psychiatric Rehabilitative Program) that provided mentoring, after school tutoring and life skills services. He told me that he could help me get more clients for my clinic if I would consider relocating to Baltimore.

He told me that the Better Project had more than 1,100 clients and that it would be beneficial to both my clinic and the Better Project. He wanted me to meet the owners of the Better Project. He went to the owners of the Better Project and told them about my services in Prince George's County. A meeting was set up for me to meet to the owners, Grover and Reese.

I met Grover and Reese. They brought the billing person who was working for their company. They said that Mike was the most competent and proficient billing person in the business. I showed Grover the approval letter to confirm that I had been approved by the state for the operation of an outpatient mental health clinic. On the letter was my provider number for billing purposes. Grover gave the letter to Mike and he made a copy of it.

Grover discussed how their company could really benefit my clinic because they had a psychiatrist that needed some help in servicing all the clients with clinical disorders. To Grover, it was an opportunity to serve more people and provide far more clinical services because with the clinic, you can provide an array of services from therapy to psychiatric evaluations and there was no limit on the number of staff that a clinic could have.

I was so elated at his proposition because for nine months I was struggling to get clients and to stay in business. I discussed with him that I had no money and could not move my business. He said, "We will take care of all the initial monies to get you acclimated and transition to Baltimore." In fact, he said he would put me on a salary until I was able to pay myself. I thought, WOW! What a great opportunity this is! God had finally answered my prayers and I could begin to do what I did best, helping the lives of people with mental health problems.

It was fall semester at the local college where I was teaching and I had to make a decision whether to return the following semester or break the contract with the school and devote 100% to operating the clinic. Grover said, "It would be extremely difficult to work at college full-time and operate the clinic, especially during its formidable stages."

As part of Grover's proposition, he and Reese would become stockholders of the clinic. They would finance all the initial monies and hire all the staff to begin the operation. We agreed that Grover and Reese would both be responsible for contributing 30% to the operation of the clinic and I would be responsible for 40% of all contributions including capital returns. So I would get 40% of all profits and Grover and Reese would both get 30% each, totally 100% for the three of us.

Now, I'm thinking this is something that I cannot turn down – a chance for my business to grow significantly, both with clients and capital gains. I was set to meet with their lawyer to finalize the deal. I agreed and decided to break my contract at the college and take the chance of a lifetime and grow my business. Upon meeting with Grover's lawyer, one of my colleagues at the college was an attorney. He and I talked about the proposed deal and I wanted him to be present at the meeting with Grover, Reese and their attorney.

At the meeting, we discussed the entire deal including a signing bonus for me. That signing bonus was $5000. According to Grover, it was a small token of appreciation for my decision to form a partnership with their business.

Their lawyer did not draw up the restrictive stock agreement after the meeting. Instead, my friend got his son, who is also an attorney, to complete the paperwork. The restrictive stock agreement was finalized and off to what I envisioned as a successful partnership in January of 2004.

The first couple of weeks, I just observed the operation of their company and how they were servicing the clients. It was amazing to see so many clinicians and so many clients getting services to help them. Everything was so organized, from the administrative staff to the outreach workers going into the communities to get referrals for service. Grover had my office set up and always made sure that I was taken care of. When I needed money for food or gas, he gave it to me. He even got me another cell phone on his business account because at the time I could not afford one.

Through my observations, everything appeared to be working out with the formation and infancy stages of my outpatient mental health clinic. I had minimum worries because Grover made sure that the clinic was fully staffed and compensated for their work.

Clinicians served as independent contractors, and many of them worked under the direction of a licensed therapist. However, in February 2004, Grover informed me that Mike was submitting the first bills in for reimbursement for my clinic's first 200 initial intakes on clients that were to be authorized for therapy services in the clinic.

It was not until the end of February that I was able to pay myself a bi-weekly salary. Up to this point, Grover paid me a check bi-weekly in the amount of $3800.

Since the clinic had just begun to get set up and provide services, it was difficult for me to get organized and learn how to effectively run the company. I knew how to be a clinician, but being in charge of so many people at one time and becoming organized was a challenge. However, I really enjoyed it. It was so exciting to see people receiving services and the rewards of those people being helped.

Here's how the operation of the clinic was supposed to operate: Referrals were sent from their company to various agencies (i.e., schools DSS, churches and community organizations). Grover had a group of outreach workers that went out into the community and solicited business to schools and inner city children. If a parent was interested in receiving services or wanted services for their child, they would come to one of the three offices and have an initial psychosocial assessment done. After that, the client would be authorized for services. Once they were authorized for service, the client would be assigned to a therapist for weekly sessions.

Once a therapist contacted a client, he could begin services and put in bills for payments. The majority of the services rendered were either intake assessment or 45-minute therapy sessions. A therapist was supposed to see a client and put a copy of the case note and bill in the client's file for recordkeeping. A copy of the bill was to be brought in and given to the billing person for submission of payment to my clinic.

To ensure that this process was done correctly, two of my employees were responsible for conducting file inspections and making phone calls as follow-up to ensure the quality of services rendered by the therapists.

In April of 2004, the other company was to undergo a series of audits to monitor their program. In fact, I even sat in on one of the audits. There was a compliance officer at the meeting and he had given Grover's company a satisfactory rating. It was Grover's suggestion to have me sit in on the audit because the clinic was scheduled to have a six-month audit shortly thereafter. It was an audit that never occurred for the clinic.

In May of 2004, Grover's company was suspended and within two weeks, they closed their program. At that time, my clinic was still currently operating and had a case load of 400 clients. I was amazed and shocked at the other company closing, but I never anticipated that we would be in any danger.

Grover and I discussed what was to happen to our partnership. He said nothing was going to happen and he knew that the other company was going to eventually closed down. He said that his focus was on keeping good ties with my clinic and me. We were doing such a remarkable job, at least in my eyes, serving the population of children and adolescents in need of mental health services.

In June of 2004, an investigator from the Office of the Attorney General's Medicaid Fraud Unit came to my house and served me with a subpoena for the submission of all records pertaining to the clinic and all business ties with the other company. I was stunned and in a state of disbelief. After all this work that I had done, my clinic was now under investigation for allegedly committing Medicaid fraud.

I thought to myself, no way! There was no way that we had committed any crime – not the way we were seeing clients, conducting staff meetings and checking therapist notes and bills to ensure everything was done correctly. We had a quality assurance system set up in my office. We checked every therapist and made random follow-up phone calls to parents of children that were being seen in the clinic.

Later in June 2004, just before the Department of Mental Health and Hygiene suspended the license of the clinic, one of my employees came to me one day and discovered some discrepancies in the billing. She said that Mike had put bills in for reimbursement, but the clients had not yet been assigned to a therapist. I carefully reviewed the discrepancies and fired Mike immediately. He had no reasonable alibi as to why he put in bills and clients had not even been assigned. I also asked him, "Who instructed you to do this?" and he stated, "No one." I immediately asked him to leave the premises before I phoned the police.

I called Grover to inform him that I had fired Mike, but for some strange reason, he begged me to bring Mike back; however, I refused. It was unethical and unprofessional for this type of nonsense and I was not going to stand for it. It was then that I realized that they had been committing Medicaid fraud the entire time that we were in a partnership.

Grover called me back and asked me if we could hire someone else. I told him that I would have to sit down and instruct him on the proper protocol for the submission of claims. I later discovered that Grover had some ties with that new worker's mother. She was the branch manager at a local bank, the same bank we did business with. He and I discussed how the bills were to be submitted – the same way in which it was always established since the beginning: therapists bring in case notes, a copy of the bill and a client tracking sheet and give it to the billing person for processing.

Approximately a week later after firing Mike and hiring someone else and talking with the investigator, my clinic was also suspended from being able to provide clinical outpatient services. We had to close down because we had no other funding source to continue paying staff and to pay overhead costs. The Attorney General's office subpoenaed all records pertaining to the clinic and all my personal banking and tax records for the past two years.

With no problem, I complied and was now out of business. One of the most interesting aspects of this whole ordeal is the outside appearance of the operation of the two businesses. It appeared to me that the other company was doing such a tremendous job that there was no reason to believe that there was any wrongdoing. There was not even a niche of talk or indication that something was going wrong.

It was the same with my clinic. Although I was the owner and president of the company, Grover brought in all the staff, financed all overhead costs, and had been in the business longer than me. It was supposed to be a learning process between the two of us. I would teach him about the care of people and he would help me to understand the infrastructure of running a business. However, it never happened. We were in business for only five months.

Ironically, I saw Grover on a couple of occasions after everything with the legal matters began. On one occasion, he accused me of stealing $60,000 from his account. We got into a big argument because, first and foremost, I was totally broke, and secondly, I never even had access to his account. Therefore, I knew that he was accusing me, but I had no way of proving it to him. Grover said that his accountant informed him of the missing $60,000 and that I must have taken it. Whatever the case may have been, they both were lying on me. I never stole anything and had no intentions of being caught up in business with corrupt people.

The second time I saw Grover was on September 12, 2006. He saw me and the first thing that he said was, "I want to apologize for accusing you of stealing money from me. I was wrong." He went on to ask me about how my family was doing and that he had heard about me being charged and said to me, "I was surprised to hear that you were charged because you did not do anything." I said to him, "Tell that to the attorney general's office." He said that my clinic was a legitimate operation and that there were never any false bills put in or any wrongdoing whatsoever.

I said to him again, "Go tell that to the attorney general's office." I went on to tell him how disappointed I was in losing the business. More importantly, not being able to service the children that were in so much need of those services was even more disappointing. He went on to say that the government was jealous that his company had made so much money in so little time that they had to investigate him. He further acknowledged that their psychiatrist was guilty because he knew that he could not have seen all those clients in one week. Grover's attitude appeared to be, "My name is not on any checks, nor did I submit any bills for any reimbursement." He went on further to note that he realized that the AG's office was after him, not necessarily the company. He was supposed to have been the mastermind behind the whole Medicaid fraud scheme.

Additionally, he said that one of his closest colleagues was the person that snitched on him and that there was a number of other witnesses that told the AG's office that he told Mike to put in bills for reimbursement. Despite all of these allegations, he denied any wrongdoing.

I do believe that he was lying to me. Like I told Grover, "I never knew of anyone putting in any false claims for payments and, I never knew of him or the other company of doing anything wrong." In fact, I never told any employee to follow any other procedure of submitting bills besides what the initial protocol was.

We departed after talking for about 15 minutes. I told him that I just wanted my name cleared and if he could tell the AG's office what he told me about not having anything to do with any wrongdoing, I would definitely appreciate it. I KNEW THAT THIS WAS NOT GOING TO HAPPEN.

Have you ever felt like your hard work, dedication and efforts became useless? I did. When I first went into private practice, I had teamed up with two business associates who were providing a very similar service as the clinic. However, the focus of their service was more rehabilitative than clinical. I was living in a small, suburban community and working at a local college teaching psychology at the time. It was a pivotal point in my life when I felt that I needed change. Have you ever felt like you needed change?

With every setback, it is an opportune time to comeback. Think back to your last setback(s) and the impact that it had both on your emotional and physical state. Depending on the severity of the setback, your emotions in most cases led you to believe that it was over and that there was no way that you could recover from the setback. And this happens all the time. Whether you experience a financial setback (job), a relationship loss (divorce) or health setbacks, you should use them to make an even stronger comeback.

You ask yourself: How can I recover when I have no plan, no motivation or spark to begin to recover? What if I can't recover? You begin to develop that self-pity talk cycle of the I can't, maybe, if, should I, rather than thinking positively and using the words I can, I will, when I do and I am. It's just a small matter of using different language and being able to verbalize how you can begin to comeback. And it simply begins with you. Take a look at the following example of how the tongue can be your worst enemy or your best antidote.

>If you keeping saying that you can't comeback
>After setbacks, you never will
>What you speak about, you can bring about,
>If you keep saying you can't stand your job,
>You might lose your job
>If you keep saying your car is garbage,
>If might break down
>If you keep saying you are broke,
>You will always be broke
>If you say you don't trust a man/woman,
>You may attract one that will always betray or hurt you
>If you keep saying you can't find someone to love and believe in you,
>Your thoughts will attract more experiences to confirm your beliefs.

My point is, turn your thoughts and conversations around to be more positive and power-packed with faith, hope, love and action. God gave you the ability to make rational decisions and choices on our own. Don't let the power of your tongue ruin what God's gift is to you. He gave it to you, so what are you going to do with it? Many of us tend to block out our talents and skills. The good thing about a setback is it forces us to take a closer look at what our gifts and abilities are and begin to capitalize on them.

Unfortunately, this was one setback that I wished was only a nightmare. It was a four-year horrible experience that nearly caused me to self-destruct. After the final investigation from the Attorney General's Office, I was charged with 42 counts of Medicaid fraud. The AG's office had enough evidence to charge me for a crime that I did not commit. I was truly a victim of circumstance.

Someone else benefited from my hard work, motivation and will to help others and used me to make millions of dollars. They lured me into an operation that appeared to be doing good community work helping children, adolescents and adults; however, they were already committing Medicaid fraud before I even became partners with that company. It was horrible.

I borrowed money from family to hire a lawyer to try and help me get my name cleared and keep me from going to jail. However, I still had to turn myself in, get fingerprinted and get processed at the local city jail. It was humiliating. I will never forget it. From the whole arrest to the processing to being released on my own recognizance led me to heavy drinking. That night before I got home, I nearly drank a bottle of Jack Daniels whiskey. In fact, as a result of the whole ordeal, I developed a serious drinking problem. I began to drink a bottle of liquor a night for nearly 18 months. It was awful. I went from depressed to a casual alcoholic in two years. Those bad habits of drinking and smoking cigars became very expensive.

I must have borrowed $10,000 total for the lawyer that I had hired to tell me he needed at least $18, 000 to cover a case of this magnitude. And when I could not borrow the remaining portion of the retainer to keep him, he made a comment to me that, "I can try to save some money now, but I may be drinking out of canteens later." He was insinuating that I would be going to jail if I did not get some good legal counsel. I was stunned. I had no other way to get any more money and time was of the essence.

The AG's office began to put pressure on my attorney to try and get me to tell what I knew about the other partners as it related to Medicaid fraud. There was one problem; I did not know anything. They camouflaged the whole operation and it was alleged that they had stolen more than $4 million in Medicaid billing. Not only was I enraged, but I felt like an idiot for allowing someone to lure me into something like this. This whole ordeal was only over a six-month period. I was in the partnership with them for only six months and was facing 20 years of prison time if found guilty.

The attorney by law had to keep me as a client until I found legal counsel. I was unable to afford a good lawyer, especially after I had already spent $10,000 and still had no results in my favor. I finally had to get a court-appointed lawyer. Hey, nothing against court-appointed lawyers, but they could give a hoot whether you go to jail or not. They are working for the state and you only have them because you cannot afford to get one.

Finally, after three years of investigation and the AG's office discovering more evidence of Medicaid fraud, they told my attorney that they would make a deal with me. It was a deal that would keep me out of jail and give me a chance to get my name cleared and continue on with my life. It all came down to me either going to trial and letting a jury decide whether they believed I had nothing to do with Medicaid fraud or taking an Alford plea. An Alford plea is pleading guilty only because the government's evidence was so strong against me that the likelihood of me winning would be slim to none. I also had a public defender who told me that she was about 50/50 on going to trial and convincing a jury that a man of my education and prior work experience was innocent; she was not sure she could win.

The AG's office told me and my lawyer to take as long as we needed to decide on what decision that I would make. And I did just that. I waited until I could not prolong it any longer. It had already been a three-year investigation and the AG's office was trying to close this case as well as the case involving the other company. They had charged Grover and Reese with Medicaid fraud for the other company, not my clinic. I was the only person that was charged with Medicaid fraud for my company. The other two partners never got charged for Medicaid fraud in my company and they were the ones responsible.

Finally, after the New Year and having taken so long with my decision, the AG's office decided to change their offer and offer me a plea bargain. That plea bargain was to accept the Alford plea and they would drop all but one of the 42 counts that they had charged me with. One count of Medicaid fraud and theft could get me at least five years in prison. My lawyer said that if we went to trial and we lost, that she could get the sentence down to maybe 18 months. I thought you got to be kidding me! First off, I was set up. Secondly, I have never stolen anything in my life. And finally, I thought that the AG's office was going to try and make an example out of me.

I thought about using the race card, but the facts were the facts. Medicaid fraud was committed in my company and I was never a part of it and never even aware of it. By taking the Alford plea, it allowed me the opportunity to have a chance to get my record cleared after my probationary period. If I had gone to trial and lost, I would have gone to jail and never been able to clear my name nor my record. It was a decision that I prayed on for another four months. I asked God to help me to make the right decision. I also asked Him to keep me out of jail so that I would not be away from my wife and kids.

I drank even more. I prayed and drank at the same time. I asked God to help me make the right decision. I was uncertain whether to take a chance and go to trial or take the plea and get on with my life. Besides, in my whole life, all I ever did was take chances and risks, some of which cost me great losses, others greater rewards.

Either way that I was to decide, I believed that God would help me to make the best decision for me and my family. And that is the way it turns out sometimes; we make decisions not just for us, but for the sake of others – in this case, my wife and kids. I never wanted to be away from them and be unable to do my duty as a father or husband if I did not have to. At one point while waiting to make the decision. I thought, hell, what do I have to lose if I go to trial?

Finally, after carefully thinking about it over and over again and asking God over and over again, I came to the decision to accept the Alford plea. It was the best decision that I felt I could live with. And, God answered my prayers to stay out of jail. And He did just that for me. He kept me out of jail. And one of the most important lessons that I had learned throughout the whole ordeal was once you ask God for help and you believe through Faith that He is going to work it out, you do not have to keep praying and asking for the same thing over and over again. In fact, if you do, you are questioning your faith in Him.

Even when the Lord blesses you, the devil tries to dampen your spirit and make things worse than they really are. I took the AG's deal and accepted the plea. As a result, I was sentenced to five years in prison and $150,000 in restitution fees owed to the state. However, God made it work out so that the judge suspended four of the five years and I was to do one year of home detention. Again, I thought to myself, you have to be kidding me. Getting the short end of a victim of circumstance appeared to becoming bleaker and bleaker as I tried to figure out how I was going to make it with a felony conviction and gain employment. So, as always when life seems so complex and you don't understand something or it seems there's no way out, leave it up to God. Through Jesus, all things are possible.

I was to wear an ankle bracelet and report to the home detention office regarding my whereabouts; including providing verification of my employment along with valid signatures to make sure I was where I said I was. I also had to pay the home monitoring system $750 a month to use the bracelet, and $150 a month to the state for restitution fees; altogether I was to pay $900 a month to keep me out of jail, move towards clearing my name and restoring my life, save my family, and comeback after such a devastating setback.

It was difficult, both financially and emotionally. For a while, I was angry at myself and those that had set me up. I kept thinking and beating myself up even though I was an innocent man. Because of the fact that I had all intentions of going into business to help others, I could not understand why I was being hurt and getting the short end of the stick.

But what I do understand today is that with every setback, God takes you through trials and tribulations to see of you are truly faithful and believe that He is going to get you through it. Even during the darkest moments that were to come, I always believed that God would make a way. I knew that He had another plan for my life, something bigger than I could ever imagine; I just didn't know what it was at that time.

My grandmother use to say, "Where there is a will, there is a way." And she literally meant that when God is involved, there will be a way. I really did not understand that statement until I became an adult and began experiencing life's setbacks and challenges.

Accepting a plea agreement meant a record of a felony conviction, something that I had never anticipated to happen in my life. After all, I had the resiliency to overcome obstacles and beat the odds that were placed upon me throughout my entire life thus far and now after accomplishing some of my goals and achievements, I was not sure how to come back after this devastating setback. I had to now figure out how to get a decent job to support my family while I discovered what it was that God wanted me to do. It was tough. The fact that I now had a criminal record caused me to be very apprehensive about applying for jobs – especially in this day and age when most employers run a criminal background check on you.

As a result of my charge and conviction, I was prohibited from working in the area of Medicaid or insurance billing, which limited my options to a minimum. All of the places that I had in mind to go after employment were either billing through Medicaid or insurance third-party billing. It literally placed me out of my career in which I had work experience and educational attainment. Not only was I embarrassed, but humiliated and ashamed of all of my life's accomplishments thus far.

As grandmother use to say, "The Lord works in mysterious ways." And He surely does. He gave me the courage and spirit to do something that I had wanted to do for more than 28 years – write a book. I had wanted to write a book that would inspire others to overcome challenges and beat the odds. And that is exactly what I did. The book's title was *Overcoming Obstacles...Beating the Odds*. It is a book that tells a story of me as a boy, who by society's standards should have been dead or in jail by the age of 18. However, through the grace of God, I was saved and a protective shield was placed over me by God so that I could live and help save the lives of others.

I wrote the book as a self-published author after being turned down from more than 100 literary agents. Writing the book also allowed me to arrange book speaking engagements and book signings as a means to bring in some cash and work for myself. Now, keep in mind that this was not my original plan; however, I now realize that it was God's plan all the time. And that is what you have to keep in mind; our plan may not be God's plan. That is why we must ask for His grace and guidance and that we must do what it is that He wants us to do.

My wife was making a decent salary working in the government and, at that time, we only had two children. Our bills were at a minimum and God made a way for us to survive. I sold books, booked my own speaking engagements, and made a living working for myself for roughly two years – one year prior to my conviction and the year while I was on home detention. And I mean it was a rough two years. My mind, body and spirit went through a daunting transformation. Both my financial and emotional state was always up and down and many times not stable. I drank alcohol to combat the emotional pain and I smoked cigars to relax my mind. And I was praying to God the whole time asking Him not to let me self-destruct. And that was exactly what I headed for – destruction.

But the one aspect of it all was my belief in God. Even the days when it seemed as if I truly was not going to make it, God gave me another day. He gave me hope, motivation and will power and showed me that through Him, all things are possible. At one time, our financial stability was so rough that my wife said, "You need to get a job. We need more money." I agreed. Selling books out of the trunk of my car and speaking for free was not enough to help out with the bills.

One day while riding down the street in Washington, D.C., God placed a spirit in me that led me to the last place that I had had a speaking engagement. It was for a government agency that had purchased more than 200 books from me and invited me to be the guest speaker for one of their graduations. I knew the program director of the agency. I stopped by one day and saw him in the parking lot. I said, "Mr. Jackson, can I talk to you for a minute?" He said yes. I told him that business was slow for me and did he have any positions for part-time work. He said, "No part time, but I do have some full-time positions available. Are you interested?" I hesitated, but replied with enthusiasm, yes! I wanted part time because I wanted to continue working for myself.

However, business was not picking up fast enough for me. I knew that this was a blessing from God and I did not want to block it; something that I think people do all the time is block their blessings and show God that they are not appreciative of those blessings. Therefore, I interviewed, was hired, and started working as a facilitator teaching life skills and job readiness classes to ex-offenders. Now who do you think really gave me that job? He made it so that there was no background check, he placed me in an area where I could use the talents he gave me, and he gave me an opportunity to have steady income. What else could I ask for? It was truly an opportunity to use the setback as a time to come back.

My setback was a test of my faith with God. I believe that God wanted to see just how much I believed in Him, so He put me through a major setback to see if I believed a comeback was possible through Him. It was based on me developing a personal relationship with God. I eventually stopped drinking and smoking cigars and began to study the Bible more and talk with God more. I asked Him to lead me in the direction in which He wanted me to go. He sent my grandmother to me in a dream. My grandmother said God told her that He wanted me to work for Him! I was stunned and scared at the same time. I was not sure in what capacity He wanted me to work in, so I prayed and prayed and prayed.

As a result, I formed another company; Angelo Reynolds Enterprises, LLC. It was formed as a family business and focused on speaking, writing books, teaching life skills to children, families and companies. I was to spread the word of God through motivation and inspiration to people all over the world. Additionally, ARE, LLC would teach life skills/job readiness to ex-offenders, the homeless and people who were unemployed and trying to transition back into the work force. It was an opportunity for me to leave my job full time and now work for God full time and all the time.

The worst thing about setbacks is you don't know when they are coming, how severe they will be, and how long they will last. The good thing about setbacks is it is truly an opportunity for a comeback. Remember this – it's not how bad the setback is it's how you handle the setback and whether you allow it to keep you from making a comeback.

Act 7

Each One Reach One
The Power of Giving Back

When I think of reaching back and giving back, there are two things that come to mind. They are our pro-social skills and our altruistic behavior. These two principles, when applied, can bring a whole new dimension to giving back. In fact, pro-social skills are nothing more than helping others and not looking for anything in return. In education, we say that people have exhibited their altruistic behaviors because they have the initiative without any acknowledgment or inquiry. These are generally the people that have exhibited such altruistic behavior their entire lives. You know the people – Big Mamma, who gives her last can of beans to a mother with three kids, even though as a result she would not be able to eat when she gave up her own food. Or Ms. Annie Mae, who lives off of monthly fixed income from SSI or government assistance and still pays her tithes and offerings to church and will give you the shirt off her back.

I have been giving back all my life. In fact, that's all I know how to do is give back. It was passed down through generations of my family. From my grandmother to my mother, giving was a part of our lives and we gave without looking for any rewards in return. My grandmother was the type of person that would give you the shirt off her back, literally. If she had it, you had it. And that is what we have to get back to – the days in which people really cared about each other and had compassion to help each other.

Unfortunately, there is something contrary to altruistic behavior and that is narcissism or the act of not giving. The practice of narcissistic behavior is not only selfish but dangerous. It is one of those practices that directly affects people in the negative form. It is the belief and practice of I got mine, now you get yours. I'm not sure where it came from, but if you are one of these people that practice this type of behavior, you are in for a rude awakening. You cannot continue to live this way. In fact, Jesus did not die on the cross and spare your life so that you could be a selfish and non-helping person.

I have always thought that the best way to bring people together is to give something back. God gave it to us, so He intended for us to do the same. In fact, it is our moral and ethical obligation as Christians and productive citizens to do so. Every time you give, you get it back, usually in abundance. So my question is: Why is it so difficult for each one to reach one?

In 2008, I was the keynote speaker for the Rev. Dr. Martin Luther King's birthday celebration for Blacks in Government (BIG) at the Internal Revenue service and the theme for the celebration was "each one reach one." When I was asked to be the speaker, I was excited; however, the topic was really what intrigued me the most. The theme "each one, reach one" is something that I have lived my entire life by. And many people talk the talk, but they rarely walk the walk. As I spoke to the audience, many agreed with everything I said. They would either respond by applauding, or by saying, "Amen, Amen." But at the conclusion of the program, a man walked up to me and said, "You know, there are many people who needed to hear what you said." He added further, "Many people love a good speech, but they realize that what you were speaking about was directly speaking to them."

I told him that I have built my entire career interest in serving others. And I know that everyone is not necessarily interested in serving or helping others, but just imagine the impact of each one reaching one. The world would be a more pleasurable place to live. There would be less homelessness, crime, violence and more opportunities for employment. If each one of us would do just that by reaching back and helping one, we truly would be in a better place. But the problem lies not in us helping each other. The problem lies in those who ask: What is in it for me? Or how can I benefit from helping this person?

And that same question has already been answered. But many of us live our lives based on short-term commitments rather than lifelong antidotes. As a society, we take the easy escape routes of doing just enough to say we did something, just enough to put a bandage on a sore that needs medication to heal carefully. And it has affected our communities (i.e., schools, churches), and most importantly, our unwillingness to exhibit the practice of collectivism. Many of our communities lack the cohesiveness and unity so strongly that it literally and profoundly breaks down many of our families.

For example, there was an incident in Washington, D.C., that involved a woman who killed all four of her children. She also stayed in the house with the children for four months before anyone had discovered the gruesome scene. But this is a prime example of what I am discussing. It was said that the children had been missing from school, that they had not been seen by the local social service agency for four months and that on several different occasions, the neighbors had indicated that the lady had knocked on their door asking for food. Here's my point – the signs should have been clear. This woman was in trouble, and the community ignored it. All that time lapsed and no one looked further into why they had not seen the woman or her children and no one called the authorities to inform them.

This is a case of no one reaching back and giving help, and as a result, four children are dead and a mother is insane. But if the community had taken the time out to closely observe that family, this probably could have been avoided; however, the community gathered around with candles after the fact in a ceremony that could have been avoided. And there are cases like this one all over the world. People not reaching out and caring for others and it results in something disastrous. There are usually many signs that lead up to incidents like this and others where people had tried to talk about their problems, but no one listened and they ended up going on a killing spree.

In fact, that was exactly what I delivered during my speech – what Martin Luther King had strived for us all to do, *"each one, reach one."* In fact, Martin Luther King gave the money he received for the Noble Peace Prize back to the communities in which he served. Now that's truly reaching back and giving back. However, we still have not learned how to do that. Or should I say practiced it so that it can impact people the way that God intended it to be?

Think back to how many times someone helped you with something. For me, if it had not been for my mother, grandmother and uncle, I am not sure where I would have ended up in life. Those family members took a keen interest in me and encouraged me to go after my dreams and aspirations. And I truly believed that is where I learned the concept of "each one reach one" and giving back. And I am so thankful that God gave those principles to my family and that they shared them and instilled those principles in me.

The act of collectivism

Today, we need to apply the concept of collectivism more than ever. That is the practice of unity, working together for a common cause, purpose and a mission in life. It is each one reach back to help one. The concept is simple – helping your family first so that you may help others later. It is such a fundamental premise; unfortunately, some people don't get it. And I am not sure if they will ever get it.

Those that practice it benefit greatly. Not only do they benefit economically, but culturally as well. It brings people together for a common cause. There's a saying I like, *"If you stand for nothing, you fall for anything."* And that is why some of our cultures are having a difficult time adapting to the new world in which we live. Historically for some cultures, the act of collectivism stood for something. Today, some have lost it and have no clue how to restore it. It is a sad thing because now the blaming game has become an alibi to try and justify the increase of crime, poverty, teen pregnancy, divorce and many more problems affecting our communities around the world.

With our children being labeled as Generation X and some of our critics and non-believers saying that our children are not our future, we have to begin to do something. We are giving up on each other. And in spite of what people say about our young folk, I still believe that God has a plan for them. Just as He had a plan for us as youngsters, He has one for them. He is sending messages, but in many instances, we ignore Him. We have to listen to our young people and stop ridiculing them for every mistake or bad choice they make. I think many of us forget that we, too, were young and did very similar things.

If a young person makes a bad choice or decision and is sent to prison, it affects us all. The same applies to the vast murders and heinous crimes being committed by our youth. We have to begin looking at these problems in the community as our problem and not their problems. You see, everything that happens in life affects us all, whether directly or indirectly. If a young person dies, that is our son or daughter that dies. The same goes for the troops that are fighting the wars in the Middle East; they are our fathers, brothers, sisters and mothers.

So why is it so difficult for people to give back? Are we so engulfed in a world that blinds the common person to extend a helping hand to a brother or sister? Or are we so self-centered and egotistic that our narcissist attitude has ruined us for life? One of the best things that we can do to please God is to give back, and not necessarily always in a monetary compensation. Time and support are fundamental principles that are priceless. If you give, you will receive. And most of the time, your blessings flourish even more than the help that you gave.

I'm not talking about giving back just to get something back. I am talking about doing it the good old way, from the kindness of your heart, where it is greatly deserved and appreciated both by you and the recipient. I can't tell you how it feels to see someone else benefit for something I did for them. I know that the person appreciated it and God sees it and makes a mental note of my diligence as a servant of Jesus. And that alone is rewarding and a great feeling.

Start thinking about ways to give back

It's never too late to start giving back. If you want to give back money because you feel like you may not have time to dedicate, then do just that. And if you are a follower of Jesus Christ and a believer in the book of Malachi 3:10, tithing is giving back a tenth of what you've earned back to God. For some people, this is controversial. I have heard some people say that they can give their 10% back to the community, while others say that according to the word of Malachi that that tenth should go back to the church. I'm not here to dispute either; however, I do believe that whatever way you decide to spend your money, that it should be truly sincere and with authentic purpose.

For those of you who have time to give back, there is a multitude of service projects that are awaiting your call. First, if you are a believer, then the basis of services is always God, then any and everything else follows. Your own church needs you. In fact, the act of collectivism is one of those cultures that still practice the act of unity. Besides, what better place and purpose than that of which stands for servicing and helping people through Christ. Because the church serves as a strong community foundation in our communities, it is inevitable and necessary to serve your church or a church first. And don't be surprised that a little time goes a long way in giving back.

For those persons who are already working and giving back to the church; it's never too late to give to an additional cause. And I'm not talking about giving and giving and not having time to help self; I am talking about sharing just some of that valuable time that we all have. There is 24 hours a day. We spend eight to 12 hours a day at work (either for someone else or for ourselves), 1 to 1½ hours commuting back and forth to work and picking up the kids. Some of us spend 30 to 60 minutes a day on exercise. And many of us can function on a minimum of five to six hours of sleep a day. Finally, on average, we are only spending about 30 to 60 minutes a night with our families. So where is the remaining time spent?

I think you get the picture and my point. Being able to maximize our time between work, family, sleep and giving back is not as complex as we think. And when you realize it, most of you spend x amount of hours doing miscellaneous things that you said you wanted to stop doing anyway (but that is another whole issue). I use this scenario of finding the time to give back as the same premise as using our brain. In fact, the human species only uses 10% of the brain. So what happens to the other 90%? I'm not sure, and there is not enough definitive research that can conclude anything concrete. But I am sure about how we waste an enormous amount of time wasting time – that is, doing nothing. And for those people, and you know who you are – the shoulda, coulda, wouldas that never amounted to anything – now is the time to stop wasting time and get motivated to give back.

For those people who are not church goers (I can't imagine that there aren't any), however, your local schools and recreation centers need you badly. The same problems that I mentioned previously are amongst our children in all our schools. And those same children are crying out for help every day. And they do so in the most effective ways – violence in schools including shootings, continued drug use and abuse, and staggering numbers of high school dropouts. Just recently, a disturbing study in Baltimore, Maryland, found that only 30% of black males are graduating from high school. That means that 70% are dropouts, possibly on drugs or are in penal institutions.

Now if that number of high school dropouts does not scare you, I'm not sure what you may be afraid of. And remember, although you may not be black or of African descent, it's not a white or black issue; it's a community issue. It is a community in which we all are a part of, a community in which we all have a moral obligation as productive citizens of our communities. You can stand back, complain, and do nothing, or you can help save our community by finding time to volunteer your wisdom, support and knowledge to people that are in their greatest need. Something as powerful as mentoring has been overshadowed and overlooked without enough positive recognition; it is truly a service that benefits the entire community.

Although I believe that many of the nations' schools have failed our children, we too have to take accountability in our roles as educators, parents and community activists to stand up to the school boards and legislators and make sure that the policies and implementation of programs are designed to bring about positive change and outcomes for all students.

And that brings me to the contrary; the school's primary job is not to raise our children, but educate them. Parents, it is our sole responsibility to instill the basic social and life skills needed for our children to attend school and be attentive enough to learn the information. In addition, we have to play active roles in our children's education – for example. Actively attending PTO meetings, parent conferences and assisting with homework and afterschool activities. As parents, we are really at the forefront in making sure our children understand the value of learning. If we don't, then who will? We have a moral and ethical obligation to make sure that we take care of our children before we can take care of others.

Why not volunteer at our detention centers?

Don't be a part of the problem, but rather an antidote to the problem. Stop talking about what should be done to those persons who have been or are incarcerated. Ask yourself where you can fit in to help out in the penal institution. I know, some of you may be saying, "I'm not going into jail and trying to help anybody." And for some of you that believe that there is not hope for people who are incarcerated, I'm here to tell you that you are absolutely right (if we don't start helping those that want a second chance in life)! Some of you act as if you never made a bad choice or decision in life, so you tend to forget that some of the things that you did almost landed you in jail or dead. So don't forget where you came from and that someone probably kept you from making bad choices and from going to jail.

Contrary to what many people think about our young people, they really do seek out and are crying out for help. The problem is, we overshadow and block out the mere fact that just a little encouragement goes a long way for someone looking for direction. I began my speaking business by volunteering at the local jails both for youth and adult populations. It was a struggle because there were many other speakers who were doing the same. And one of the concerns for many of the institutions was the same ole' song and dance that was being delivered. I had to take a slightly different turn and speak more from a spiritual teaching and inspirational approach.

You don't have to be a minister to go and volunteer what you know and what experiences you have in life and share it with someone else. Just imagine how powerful it would be if each person (OK, even every other person in the world) did that. Imagine the impact that it would have on reducing the incarceration rate among all people! I know, it seems like a large dream, but I do believe in making dreams a reality. And that is what you can do to help those who are incarcerated. Remember this –

every effort taken is a step closer to solving some of the problems in all of our communities.

Act 8
Use the Past as a Catalyst for Your Future

God is the maker of all created reality, including the reality of our personal lives. He knows every aspect of our lives, from conception to death. He also knows when we will fail, experience setbacks, and face the challenges and obstacles in life. God is a God of truth who knows, understands, and can make statements that correspond to the reality of our personal lives.

Since God is the God of all truth, an authentic follower of Jesus Christ will love not only God but also all truth that God knows and understands. An authentic believer of Jesus will welcome all truth relevant to his personal life – be it regarding his mind and heart, his emotions, his thoughts, or his choices – that will help him live more obediently and more wisely before God.

Some people, however, are reluctant to look closely at their past. I always tell people not to allow their past to dictate their future. However, over the years I realized your past can serve as a catalyst for your future. It can serve as a reminder that you may not want to relive the past and also be a motivator to help you move forward and not backwards in life. It can be a safeguard towards future danger and serve as an armor to shield the perils of the world. Use your life challenges, setbacks, obstacles and tribulations to help serve you and others in need of help. Just as God allowed you to survive the past, it's your turn to give those blessings to others. Don't be selfish, the world is truly not all about you; if it were, then you would be in charge and not God.

Whether you had a traumatic childhood experience or not, we all have had life experiences that we imagined could ruin our lives. But the underlying question that I ask you is: How is your past being used as a catalyst for your future? Are you like many people, ignoring or shadowing your past? Many people realize that they have made it this far not by chance, but merely by faith and the grace of God. And even though many of us in the past have strayed away from the past, it surfaced back for us in various times in our lives. Nevertheless, they were times when in reality we should have been dead or abandoned with nowhere to go, or those times when you literally felt as if you were going insane. And most of the time you were.

We all have had these feelings of inequities about our past; however, what have or will you do about it? Are you going to continue to make excuses as to why you have not achieved your goals and the level of success in your life? How long are you going to use the excuse that you came from a dysfunctional family? And finally, how many times are you going to say, "You don't understand"? Now is the time to believe that you can and will achieve what you desired. And no, it won't be easy, but the best is still yet to come.

Frequently people interpret references to "being a new creature in Christ" and "forgetting what lies behind" as meaning that their personal past is in no way relevant to their new lives as believers. Consequently, they conclude that to explore their personal past would demonstrate a lack of faith in God. I disagree. I believe that for some, it's painful and they don't want to face it. I do believe that people desire to be rid of their past and be able to move forward in their lives, they just need help.

In the "new creature" passage (II Corinthians 5:11-19), Paul is making the case for the ongoing transformation of his motives, mindset and actions that began at his conversion. He is not saying that his pre-conversion experiences are irrelevant. In the "forgetting what lies behind" passage of Philippians 3:1-21, Paul is discounting his past religious and moral achievements as well as his physical lineage as a means of making himself worthy of God's approval and justification, but he is not suggesting there is nothing helpful about learning from his past.

In fact, in Philippians 3:6-9 and Galatians 1:13-14, Paul described his past in not-so-glowing terms in order to explain more clearly the miraculous and radical effect the gospel and the work of God has had on him. The truth of his past helps him better understand his present, and the truth of his present helps him better understand his past.

If, in these passages, Paul, the divinely inspired author, is not discouraging his readers from looking at or learning from their past, why have some people interpreted them this way?

One possible explanation is because exploring one's past can be a very uncomfortable process, so much so that sincere Christians have used a misinterpretation of the Bible to substantiate the belief that their personal past is irrelevant. As uncomfortable as the process of looking at our past might be, however, exploring and understanding the truth regarding our past may help us accurately interpret the present and live wisely in the future. All truth is God's truth and worth knowing and understanding in an appropriate manner, especially as it relates to our personal lives and destinies.

The metaphor of a lens can help us think through the value of this process. We all perceive our personal lives through an internal lens, which is the set of beliefs we use to interpret reality. We construct this lens as we proceed through our lives, gathering data about ourselves and about the world around us. As Christians, we use two main sources of data to construct our lenses: (1) our life experiences with people (going back to childhood) and (2) the Bible. Both play significant roles in determining what we have come to believe about ourselves and the world around us. Through this set of beliefs, this lens, we interpret our current experiences and make choices that develop into our future.

The biggest problem with our personal lens is sin. Sin inextricably distorts our lens such that our perception of ourselves and the world around us can be severely blurred. Consequently, we can make very self-destructive choices that lead not only to considerable frustration and pain but, if unchecked by God's grace, to divine condemnation in the next life.

For example, in Luke 18:9-14 Jesus tells a parable "to certain ones who trusted in themselves that they were justified" before God. The parable describes a Pharisee whose sin has distorted his lens. Looking at himself through his corrupted lens wrongly informs him that he can make himself worthy of God's blessing by his religious and moral pursuits. As a result, the Pharisee thanks God because he believes he is not sinful like other people. However, Jesus declares him arrogant and condemned before God. The Pharisee's internal lens has distorted his perception such that he has viewed himself and his relationship to God inaccurately.

Sin can also blind us to the fact that our lens is distorted. Our natural rebelliousness against truth and reality often prevents us from closely examining our lens and challenging our beliefs. Even after becoming a Christian, when God has begun to reshape our lens by "opening our eyes" to the fact that we are sinners who desperately need His grace, we will still struggle with sin; sometimes we will still hide from the truth, especially the painful truth of seeing ourselves accurately. To know all relevant truth, we must not only study the Bible and examine the world around us, but we must also simultaneously examine our personal lives. Exploring the lens we use to interpret our experiences may involve an appropriate examination of our past in order to discover the specific nature and details of our beliefs. The more honestly and clearly we do so, the better able we will be to focus our lens to God's truth from the Bible and to live more obediently and wisely before God.

In the Sermon on the Mount, Jesus describes a hypocrite who is eager to remove the speck of dust from his brother's eye but fails to notice the log that is in his own eye (Matthew 7:1-5). Because sin distorts the lens through which we interpret our life experiences, our sin can prevent us from viewing ourselves accurately while we think we see other people's sin very accurately. The man with the log in his eye is self-deceived; the log of self-righteousness has distorted his perception of himself. Dealing with the log in our eyes can be very uncomfortable, and thus we naturally tend to avoid the internal conflict of seeing ourselves impartially. Fortunately though, God is gracious and committed not only to our noticing the log in our own eye, but also to our dealing with it in an honest and thorough manner; He is at work in our lives to give us "eyes to see" the truth about Him, about ourselves and about others.

Because the work (and indeed, it can be arduous labor) of exploring and challenging the lens that affects our decisions can be painfully overwhelming, some Christians choose to continue living with an inaccurate lens. But as believers in the gospel committed to all relevant truth, our personal comfort must be secondary to truth, even the truth of our past and our uncomfortable emotions. Jesus confronted this kind of resistance to truth when He said to the Pharisees in Luke 5:33-39, "No one after drinking old wine wishes for new, for he says, 'The old is good enough.'" Jesus could just as easily have said, "No one after looking through a misshapen lens wishes to reshape it, for he says, 'The existing shape is good enough.'"

Let me give an example of how one's misshapen lens can affect one's life. My Christian friend, John, believes from his childhood experiences that he is wholly unlovable and not valuable. His study of the Bible seems to confirm that he is unlovable because he is fundamentally a sinful rebel against God. But John also believes from his study of the Bible that God loves him according to His grace and considers him valuable enough that Jesus Christ died for him as an instrument of His mercy. Of course, John's belief that God loves him should overwhelm his belief that he is unlovable, thus appropriately reshaping his internal lens.

Unconsciously, however, John continues to respond to his beliefs from his childhood by overachieving in his job, in his marriage and in his relationships with others. He does this because he believes that if he works hard enough in all these areas and performs well enough, God will consider him lovable and valuable on the basis of his performance. In addition, he believes that if he performs well enough before God, God will reward him by (1) taking away his seemingly insatiable need for love and (2) relieving his depression and loneliness. But none of this has happened yet, and so John constantly redoubles his efforts and wonders why God has not fully rewarded him and why he still feels a lack of acceptance and approval from others and from himself.

John's lens is distorted. He is unable to integrate his continued sinfulness with God's constant love and grace towards him. His experientially derived beliefs from childhood are colliding with his biblically derived beliefs. In spite of his biblical belief in God's gracious love, his internal belief that he is wholly unlovable and not valuable blurs his vision. He naturally responds to this belief by trying to prove himself valuable by working extra hard at being a good person.

When he fails in any way to meet God's standard of righteousness, he views himself as unlovable and not valuable and he descends into the depths of depression repeating the cycle over and over again. John needs to seek the truth about him. He may find it helpful to explore his past experiences and his present emotions as a means of discovering the genesis of his current blurred lens.

Through this process, he may be able to challenge his false beliefs and compare them with what the Bible declares as true. Even though John may again act out of his false beliefs, this process may give him a better framework within which to understand himself and thereby take responsibility for his behavior as well as his motivations.

If, like John, we are unaware of our experientially derived internal beliefs, then we may have difficulty knowing how these beliefs are interacting with our biblically derived beliefs to shape our lens. For example, if I believe God is a loving and forgiving heavenly Father, but my childhood experience tells me fathers are hard and abusive, I might tend to relate to others and to myself on the basis of the latter and not the former. My experientially derived beliefs may overwhelm my biblically derived beliefs, especially when I relate to people in authority over me.

The past is relevant to the present and plays an important role in my building the lens through which I perceive and interpret life. Understanding the past and its effect on my lens can be a great help to me, not only in reshaping my lens, but also in living more obediently and wisely before God. Regrettably, some Christians believe that to explore in depth any painful past experiences is "living in the past" and indicates a lack of faith in God.

On the contrary, *we live in the past* when we resist understanding our experientially derived beliefs and how they play themselves out in our lives. We can become stuck in destructive behaviors; for example, overachieving to gain God's approval, which (1) leads to increased frustration and pain, and (2) reinforces our erroneous belief that we are wholly unlovable and not valuable. With or without intention, we can fail to believe and trust God for what He is doing in our lives – namely, leading us away from being legalistic overachievers and towards being loving, biblical achievers.

Being open to the truth, including truth about our personal lives (past and present, inside and outside, experiential and biblical), is vital for our spiritual, mental, emotional and psychological health now and our eternal well-being in the future. If our sin is preventing us from pursuing any aspect of this truth, we must repent, embrace God's mercy, and forge ahead by His grace. No matter how difficult or painful any part of this truth-seeking process might be, whether with respect to our personal lives or to the Bible, seeking the truth is more important than our personal comfort and holding onto our preconceived notions. Constantly pursuing truth in order to reshape our lens ultimately leads to authentic love for God and others and to eternal life.

Act 9

Do You!

Don't give up five minutes before the miracle happens. This happens a lot. People get tired, frustrated, and lose faith and belief in self. They sometimes forget to take care of self first. They spend the vast majority of their time helping others and less time on what's going to help them. They look around and realize that their relentless efforts of helping others were a good deed, but they have not helped themselves. I'm definitely not against helping people but there comes a time when you have to take a stand. The only way the devil wins is if you stop fighting. Nothing and no one can come between you and what God has in stored for you. I don't care who they are and what they say to you. You have to do you!

That means taking care of you before you take care of others. I know, it's selfish; but sometimes you have to be selfish. If you can't do for you, how are you going to do for others? In order to help others, you must first take care of yourself – not by being self-indulgent, but by loving yourself. Charity begins at home, and that is a realistic kind of attitude.

If you strive to keep your mental and physical well being in good condition, you will then be able to help others if they are in need – could be family, friends or close associates. Not caring about you does not lend itself, in any way, to providing tangible or intangible assistance to anyone else. Keeping yourself ready to run, so to speak, for the purpose of being in charge of your own well being, will insure that you are mentally and physically capable of meeting any challenge.

How will you be able to provide help for a friend who wants to quit smoking if you can't quit yourself? First you – then, take care of everybody else. A good message to send to you would be, "I care," which could go a long way in starting the process of having healthy self-love, then onto the rest of the story. Be good to yourself, as much as you possibly can, every day of every year. Here are a few helpful tips useful as you Do You!

Physical

"For ye are bought with a price; therefore, glorify God in your body, and in your spirit, which are God's."
– I Corinthians 6:15-20

God has invested in you. So why don't you invest in you? You have talents, thoughts, abilities, gifts (both naturally born God-given and power from on high in the Holy Spirit), financial help, time, energy, and opportunities, and just as the parable says, we will be held accountable for how we have invested these "securities." Many of these gifts from God are carried by your physical body – after all, it is your means of conveyance, how you communicate, how you are seen, how you do and think and feel. Pastor Rick Warren could not have said it better, "Worship is far more than praising, singing, and praying to God. Worship is a lifestyle of *enjoying* God, *loving* Him and *giving* ourselves to be used for His purposes. When you use your life for God's glory, everything you do can become an act of worship." If you are unsure, go to God's words for answers.

Go to God's word. He tells you how to please Him, what is appropriate for your body and for your mind, and what is definitely NOT appropriate. Read the Bible. Don't go to false teachers that say it is fine to be a "carnal Christian," a drunkard or defiler or reprobate or delinquent or criminal or glutton or lascivious – it matters what you DO with your body, including being very, very careful with unhealthy foods, narcotics, alcohol and activities, and even thoughts. For a long time, I also struggled with this. You have to be careful about what advice you get from people. As my grandmother would always say, "You can't be a fair-weather Christian." It's either all or nothing.

Your body is truly your temple! Get moving! Move your body, whether on a team sport or regular exercise (that we should be doing anyway) or just dancing, stretching (yoga) or walking over to the park to feed the ducks. Give your body something good to eat that doesn't come in a bag or box from a drive-through. Cook it yourself. Take time for yourself, not just whatever is the fastest thing. Get the message or something to wear that has great texture and color.

There are many examples throughout the Bible of people who put God's will first when it came to diet and nutrition. In the first chapter of Daniel in the Bible, Daniel said he was going to deny the delicacies of the day. "God gave him extra wisdom, strength, and favor," Shepherd says. "He didn't say 'I'm going to go on a great diet of low carbohydrates, take this diet pill so I can have the best body in the kingdom'."

Forget about the New Year's resolutions to eat better and exercise regularly. They are often short-term promises that lead to long-term failures. Instead of setting yourself up by following diets, *change* your eating lifestyle. Start eating more fresh vegetables, baked and broiled food, less red meat, and focus on fish, lean turkey and whole grains and whole wheat breads. Believe me, it makes an incredible difference in the way you feel and look. Cut out all the refined sugars and focus on the natural sugars found in your fruits.

I know this may sound like repeated information. You've heard it on TV, in fitness magazines and from diet gurus. Remember, we are discussing change and the actions that you take to make those changes. Change is not following a diet that everyone else does. Change is doing what others usually can't and won't do.

3 John 2 says, "Beloved, I hope that you are in good health — may you thrive in all other ways as you do in the spirit." God's word also tells us to give our bodies as a living sacrifice to the Lord (Romans 12:1) — and it's a sacrifice to give up food that we crave," she says. "God's word [also] tells us that our body is the temple where the Holy Spirit dwells" (I Corinthians 6:19).

Men, go to the doctor when you are sick. Many times we wait until it's too late or we have been diagnosed with an illness. Many diseases are preventable when you use preventative measures. Now God gave you the body, but it's still up to you to take care of it.

Mental/Emotional

Don't be so hard on yourself. We can be our own worst enemies. Find the positives and stop focusing on the negative. Mental illness is one of the major health problems in our society. It has been estimated that at least half of those persons in hospital beds are there for no organic reason, but because they have emotional problems. Some medical research has concluded that, "Medical science recognizes that emotions such as fear, sorrow, envy, resentment and hatred are responsible for the majority of our sickness. Estimates vary from 60% to nearly 100%". Some psychologists suggest that, mentally, people fall into three general classes.

1. Normal – These people experience their share of daily problems, get tired, are angry on occasion, and have their ups and downs.
2. Neurotic – He is able to live in society and work around other people. However, these people often experience anxiety. These people may be hypochondriacs and imagine they are seriously ill.
3. Psychotic – This person has an emotional disorder that is so severe he requires custodial care. He has lost touch with reality and may be subject to delusions or hallucinations. He sometimes completely

withdraws from society and does not respond to others around him. He tends to live in a world of his own.

Some causes of emotional disturbance include:

A. Sometimes the origin of these disturbances is organic, hormonal or chemical. Persons affected in this manner need medical attention.

B. Genetic defects, degenerative changes that accompany advanced age, the use of alcohol and other drugs can precipitate physical alterations in the brain that manifest themselves in emotional trauma. As with the first group, these people often require medical attention.

C. However, not all mental problems are genetic or organic in origin. People's emotional problems are oftentimes spiritual problems that have been allowed to go unresolved. They have been allowed to escalate to the point where these people simply cannot enjoy a happy, fulfilled life. These people become a misery to themselves and to those around them. Persons who suffer from emotional problems caused by spiritual problems do not need the advice of modern psychologists or psychiatrists, nor do they need drug treatment.

D. Sin places an enormous emotional toll on those who sin. Consider the following:
1. Sin <u>separates</u> a person from being of absolute purity, which is God (Isaiah 59:1-2). No one can enjoy true happiness as long as he is separated from his Creator.
2. Sin <u>saddens</u>. The prodigal son was in a state of depression until he "came to himself" and was reunited with his father (Luke 15:11ff).
3. Sin <u>scars</u>. Even when a person knows he has been forgiven of his sin, he may continue to carry the burden of his sin. Long after his conversion, Paul referred to himself as the "chief of sinners" (I Timothy 1:15).

4. Sin <u>sours</u>. Carrying the burden of sin can cause a person to become negative and critical – "misdirected hostility."

5. Sin <u>sickens</u>. Sin can produce heart problems, ulcers, and emotional difficulties.

6. Sin <u>sears</u>. When sin is left uncorrected, it allows the heart to become hardened. Paul spoke of those who were "past feeling" (Ephesians 4:19).

Spiritual problems have spiritual solutions

- Modern psychiatry/psychology is sometimes unable to deal with man's problems. Although I do encourage that you seek the psychological help if you need to.
- Modern psychiatry/psychology is often theory and can be less pragmatic.
- Modern psychiatry/psychology often strives to be morally neutral and refuses to make judgments concerning values.
- There is only one solution to those emotional problems that are spiritually caused. That solution is God's word (II Peter 1:3).
- The Bible is the best psychology textbook in the world. The Bible not only diagnoses humanity's weaknesses, it also provides the cure.

Just as Jesus restored (through the miraculous) soundness of mind to the demoniac, he can restore soundness of mind (through his word) to those who have emotional problems due to spiritual lapses. Don't be so hard on yourself. Become more accepting, kind and easy to forgive yourself and others. How would you treat a good friend who needed some emotional support? Take every other "I should" out of your vocabulary and say "no" at least once a week! You will appreciate it in the long run even when others don't. Create reasonable expectations. Remember, change does not happen overnight. This doesn't mean the end of motivation or working hard. The point is to stretch you, not break yourself. Set limits if that is what you need; overindulgence is not nurturing either.

Get enough people in your life that you can laugh with, share a movie or sporting event with, talk to seriously (in confidence) when an occasion comes up, who respect you and don't expect you to do all the work of keeping up the friendship or relationship. Do a variety of things for fun and stimulation, some that you can do with others and some to do alone. Having trouble coming up with an idea? Remember things you liked when you were a child, but have long ago given up. Get the creative juices flowing? Paint, draw, get out the hammer and nails and construct something.

Spiritual

Develop a practice that exercises your mind and soul. Trust me; it makes a whole world of difference. You can define that however you wish, whether it is a routine of prayer, meditation or attending services that build up your spirit and faith with like minded others; exploration of yourself that helps you to identify your values and priorities; reading wisdom literature and discussions with others that deepens your knowledge of yourself and the universe, or finding a way to contribute to the well being of others. Here are four spiritual laws that will be useful to you.

1. God loves you even when you or someone else stops. God will always love you – forever! Remember, He gave His only son for our sins so we could live. Do you know anyone else who will love you unconditionally as He? I don't. So the question that I ask you today is: Why is it that most people are not experiencing the abundant life that God has for them? You have to seek Him! The Bible teaches us to draw closer to Him and He will draw closer to you. Ask and ye shall receive. Trust me, it works! Better yet, trust Him and reap the everlasting rewards.
2. Remember, man is sinful; therefore, never put all of your trust in him. If you do, you will fail every time. In fact, God should be a part of every decision you make in life. Ask Him if you are making the right decision. He has a way of showing us, but we have to be receptive and open to His decisions, otherwise we think we solve it on our own, which is impossible. Think for a moment of the times that you had to make decisions about jobs, family, friends, relationships, finances, etc. And remember when things did not turn out the way you planned it? I know, you are smart and know how to make decisions, but think of how better

it would be if you included Him in the process. God never fails or makes bad decisions; it just doesn't happen on our accord. The Bible also teaches that most of us are stubborn and have this self-ill will that we can do things alone.

3. Jesus Christ is the only provision for man's sins. Once you know and accept Him, you will begin to experience the glory of what He has in stored for you. Jesus is the only way to get to God. He said it so eloquently, "I am the truth, and the life; no one comes to the Father but through me".
4. Since God is a jealous God, we must be narcissistic and accept Jesus Christ as Savior and Lord; then we will know and begin to experience God's love for our lives. This is one of those times when you have to be selfish. No matter what anyone accepts, your acceptance of Jesus is for you. Don't worry about what others think or accept; your acceptance is building a covenant with Him. How do we receive Him? Through faith, personal invitation, prayer and worship, and repenting of our sins. God knows your heart and is not concerned with your words as He is with your attitude. Remember earlier in this book when I mentioned attitude is everything? Here is an example of what I say when I talk to God:

> *Heavenly Father, I come to you merciful and graciously. I ask for your forgiveness and your direction. I need you. The tasks and decisions I am about to make, I cannot make them alone. I need you to guide me into the direction in which you want me to go. Have mercy on those who will reject my cause and purpose. For I know that you have greater things in stored for me. Make me the person that you want me to be. I thank you for all that you have done and continue to do for me and my family. Bless those that are struggling to develop a covenant with you for it is a daily battle with the worldly forces. I ask in your name I pray to you the God of all Gods, in Jesus' name, Amen.*

Once you have prayed and asked for God's help, you don't have to ask Him again. I hear people saying that they are praying for the same things over and over again. God heard you the first time. When you keep praying the same prayer over and over again, you are questioning if God is going to make a way for you. He heard you the first time. Never question your faith! If you say you believe, then show God that you believe and leave it alone.

Some people may say that to *do you* may appear to be a form of narcissism; that is, a sense of arrogance and egotistical attitude that it's all about you. Remember this – if it's to be, it's up to me! To a certain degree, I agree. Listen, to be successful in this world means you have to make sacrifices. You can't be at two places at the same time. There's only 24 hours in one day. Therefore, your time is divided between doing you (going after your goals), spending time with your family, and if you are employed, your employer. Something has to give. Hopefully, you are surrounded by people who understand and respect what you are trying to do (good luck with that one).

The great thing about *doing you* is accountability. You are accountable to you if you give up. The blaming game begins and ends with you. Now, when you point to someone to blame, you have three other fingers pointing right back. Although I was an innocent person during my legal problems, I had to ask myself several times: Was I naïve? What should I have been more careful about when going into business with people I did not know? And more importantly, what lessons did I learn so that I will not make those same mistakes again? That's being accountable. Even when you are the fall guy or it truly was not your fault, somewhere you have to be held accountable. Think back for a moment when you were faced with a situation that was truly out of your control. Now think about the role you could have played in preventing that situation.

Doing you is the only excuse you have to not make it. I can't, maybe, if and can I? Have to be turned into I will, I can, etc. If not, you may end up being the shoulda, coulda, woulda person that never amounts to anything. You begin to reflect on what you could have done, what woulda happened if you did, and shoulda that you were afraid to do back then. This kind of thinking is absolutely reckoning thinking and should be prohibited at all times.

No one is going to be able to *do you* but you. Remember this – most people are not sharing your dreams and aspirations, nor do most people truly believe that you can be what you want to be. You don't have time to waste worrying what someone thinks of you or what you are trying to do. It's all about being focused and not letting the worldly forces take over the Godly forces.

Conclusion

I hope what I have shared with you becomes vital information that will assist you with change. Change is continuous, infinite and everlasting. Those that are able to make the necessary changes in their lives will be the most productive and successful in whatever they do in life. God has the first and last say and has planned an abundance of prosperity and joy for us; you just have to ask and seek Him. He will never leave you or forsake you. Trust and believe that any change that you do, He will make it happen for you. Put Him first and you'll never go wrong. That's not to say that life's challenges and obstacles won't come your way, but when they do, you will be better equipped to handle them.

Time will wait for no one. Start right now to begin making those small changes that will lead to great rewards. Stop doubting yourself and listening to the negative people around you; remember, man will fail you every time and if you fail to plan – plan to fail! If you haven't included God in your transformation to change, immediately begin to do that. Continue to focus on the solutions rather than the problem itself. When you worry, you question your faith. Ask God for it once, and leave it alone. Praying over and over, louder and louder is not going to get your prayers answered faster. God is going to answer your prayers when He deems it's time, not because we feel like we deserve it or that it's our time to get it.

I also would like to encourage you to continue to stay focused and on the path of your goals, aspirations and dreams. Even when you think no one is in your corner, God is always there. We may never understand God's plans but rest assured; we should include Him with them. I never thought after all the endeavors, accomplishments and various careers that I held that I would become a speaker on personal development. It was never in my plan. However, God had planned it for me all along; it just took me to be receptive to His messages and stop being so stubborn by trying to do things my way.

Finally, just as faith is useless without work, likewise change is not attainable without action. You can talk the talk, but are you willing to walk the walk? Remember, the best is yet to come! May the blessings of God be yours.

Made in the USA
Charleston, SC
19 June 2014